About Demos

Who we are
Demos is the think tank for everyday democracy. [...]
be able to make personal choices in their daily li[...]
common good. Our aim is to put this democrati[...] [...]ing
with organisations in ways that make them more effective and legitimate.

What we work on
We focus on six areas: public services; science and technology; cities and public
space; people and communities; arts and culture; and global security.

Who we work with
Our partners include policy-makers, companies, public service providers and social
entrepreneurs. Demos is not linked to any party but we work with politicians
across political divides. Our international network – which extends across Eastern
Europe, Scandinavia, Australia, Brazil, India and China – provides a global
perspective and enables us to work across borders.

How we work
Demos knows the importance of learning from experience. We test and improve
our ideas in practice by working with people who can make change happen.
Our collaborative approach means that our partners share in the creation and
ownership of new ideas.

What we offer
We analyse social and political change, which we connect to innovation and
learning in organisations. We help our partners show thought leadership
and respond to emerging policy challenges.

How we communicate
As an independent voice, we can create debates that lead to real change.
We use the media, public events, workshops and publications to communicate
our ideas. All our books can be downloaded free from the Demos website.

www.demos.co.uk

First published in 2006
© Demos
Some rights reserved – see copyright licence for details

ISBN 1-84180-164-X
Copy edited by Julie Pickard
Design by Ispeaktoyou
www.ispeaktoyou.co.uk
Illustrations by Claudia Boldt
www.claudiaboldt.com
Printed by Upstream, London

For further information and
subscription details please contact:

Demos
Magdalen House
136 Tooley Street
London SE1 2TU

telephone: 0845 458 5949
email: hello@demos.co.uk
web: www.demos.co.uk

About this pamphlet

This pamphlet grew out of a series of conversations about projects in our respective organisations. We realised that many of the organisations we were working with – Demos in the public sector and Engine in the private sector – faced a similar set of challenges around the provision of great service. This led us to explore whether or not there are some common principles of service innovation.

The Journey to the Interface brings together what Demos and Engine have learnt from working with service organisations, along with the contributions of over 50 professionals from private, public and voluntary organisations and a number of independent experts in service design. The purpose of the pamphlet is to bring together and organise some of the language and concepts of user-centred service. We have couched this work in the context of the priorities for public service reform in coming years.

We hope that the pamphlet provides a useful resource for service organisations, as well as a conceptual framework for approaches to reform. In that spirit, each of the core chapters (1, 2 and 3) concludes with a set of challenges – questions people can ask to test the extent to which their organisation is focused on creating deep relationships with their users – and some shared language for service innovation. After each of these chapters you will find case studies of public service organisations that are putting some of the principles described here into practice. And at the end of the pamphlet there is a glossary – a 'shared language of service' – that summarises the new concepts we introduce here.

Although many of the tools and concepts described here can be applied to existing organisations, the transformative potential of service design as an approach really comes to life only if it is applied at a systemic level. After the concluding chapter, which explores this in more depth, you will also find an agenda for action that describes what service design principles and practice might might mean for people operating at different levels of the system.

We welcome your contributions to this work as it develops. Do get in touch.

Sophia Parker
sophia.parker@demos.co.uk

Joe Heapy
joe@enginegroup.co.uk

Contents

Chapter 3
Measuring success

Find ways of measuring experiences as well as systems: life is more complicated than a key performance indicator.

Measure success obsessively, but not through operational efficiency alone. Two other crucial dimensions include success in terms of reducing 'failure demand' (the cost of not getting things right the first time), and success in harnessing the underused resource of people's energy and commitment.

Chapter 4
The politics of service design

If applied systemically, service design can offer a vision for the transformation of public services, as well as a route to get there.

Don't let existing organisational boundaries limit demand. Find new ways of supporting and investing in the 'in-between spaces' through the formation of partnerships and social enterprises where new models of service have a chance to develop. Make the systemic challenge one of scaling up these approaches.

An agenda for action

Just as outcomes need to be co-produced, so does transformation: how service design principles can be applied at every level of the system, from local authorities and policy-makers to politicians.

A shared language of service

There is a small but growing discipline of service design. This glossary brings together key tools and concepts of this discipline to create a shared language of service that cuts across all sectors.

prepare at home

Introduction
The common challenge of service

From cleaning the streets to checkouts, from looking after our elderly parents to selling us holidays, more than 20 million people in the UK work in service. The so-called 'service economy' now makes up 72 per cent of our GDP.[1] Most of us work in service; all of us depend on it for many aspects of our existence. The giving of service and the receiving of it is an unmistakable part of everyday life.

Yet the shift to a service economy has not necessarily heralded a service revolution. Many of our interactions with service organisations are characterised by profound frustration, hanging on the end of a phone, arguing over our consumer rights, feeling ignored and misunderstood, worrying about the working conditions of those who serve us. Too often as recipients of services we feel that someone other than us is benefiting. Too often it feels like 'producer interests' or profit incentives matter more than how we feel.

Public services are not exempt from this sense of frustration. Since 1997, the public sector has expanded. Public service jobs have grown, as have the levels of investment being poured into our schools, hospitals, cultural institutions and security infrastructure. NHS spending will be 90 per cent higher in 2007/08 when compared with 1996/97. Schools spending will be 65 per cent higher and transport will be 60 per cent higher.[2] Yet these investments are doing little to shift the stubborn figures which indicate that we still have low levels of satisfaction and trust in public services overall.

Two problems lie at the heart of this disconnect between people and services. First, people are changing faster than organisations are. Decades of expanding choice and growing wealth have left people looking for more than simply quality products and services. The search for meaning and recognition, autonomy and control is a defining part of our collective psyche in the twenty-first century. The second problem is that 'service' is still seen as a commodity rather than as something deeper, a form of human interaction. Many large organisations still seek to provide service for the lowest cost and maximum profit. This, we argue, eats away at the fundamental purpose of service: to provide support and to help people live their lives to their full potential.

This pamphlet makes the case for acknowledging the *common* challenge of service in thinking about how to transform public services. Starting here leads to a different diagnosis of the problem. It is not that public services need to be more like commercial service providers. It is that *all* service organisations need to find new ways of connecting intimately with their users and customers, of listening and responding in ways that reassure us all that we are being understood. In order to develop our thinking we spent time with a wide range of organisations – from all sectors: public, private and voluntary – that appear to be making inroads in building strong relationships with customers and users. Drawing on the interviews, workshops and case studies we conducted, we have generated a set of service design principles – practical tools and concepts – that offer fresh approaches to organisations seeking to close the gap between what they do and what people want and need.

The current managerialist narrative about public service reform is out of sync with what people want and need from services at precisely the time that a febrile political environment is awakening a fresh debate about how people and services should relate to one another. Progressive politicians urgently need to create a vision for public services that puts people and places, not targets and key performance indicators (KPIs), at its heart. But if people are going to believe this vision, equally urgent is the need to refresh and renew the approaches that are taken to public service transformation.

In this pamphlet we argue that this common challenge, facing all service organisations, leads to two major consequences. First, learning how to create deeper forms of satisfaction and wellbeing through service is the long-term priority for public service reform. Second, a distinctive approach to 'service design', which seeks to shape service organisations around the experiences and interactions of their users, presents a major opportunity for the next stages of public service reform: a route to get there.

The search for real meaning

For many people, relative material comfort is no longer enough. Twenty years ago, when asked what people looked for when making purchases, the most common response was 'quality of product'. In 2004 the most common answer was 'honesty'.[3]

The result of the massive expansion in material wealth is that, in Ulrich Beck's words, 'people demand the right to develop their own perspective on life and to be able to act upon it'.[4] The search for meaning, for authenticity, amid a world of brands, competing messages and demands, now characterises the lives of many people in affluent western economies.

As one of the interviewees for this project put it, 'we are tired of being treated as nobodies with no personality by monolithic institutions, we want to be recognised and understood.' And as Michael Willmott and William Nelson argued in their book *Complicated Lives*, 'the self is now something we seek to understand and express, not something we simply accept. This raises difficult issues for individuals as well as our companies and public services who are still struggling to escape the historical legacy of mass provision.'[5]

As employees and citizens, we're tired of working and want our work–life balance; as consumers we're impatient of being nameless and faceless, fighting for our needs; we want relationships not transactions; we want real voice not meaningless choice. Shoshana Zuboff and Jim Maxmin have argued that the sheer scale of the social and economic shifts of the last century, combined with the new possibilities offered by technology, add up to a wholly new enterprise model.[6] In this model, it is not products or services that we value most: it is support. Support that helps people to lead their own lives as they wish, and support that helps us to navigate an increasingly complex and information-laden world where it is hard to know who to trust.

The commodification of service

Imagine signing up to a luxury sports and leisure club. In exchange for a significant monthly fee, you are able to attend unlimited sessions, use as many large soft towels as you wish, pick and choose from a range of treatments and relax in the social area. Imagine if, one day, you visit to find a large notice limiting each customer to just one towel each. When you go to the reception desk to enquire about something, you notice a printout charting profits per month over the last quarter. The prices of refreshments have suddenly gone up and you notice that a treatment that had once lasted a luxurious hour now takes only 40 minutes.

Good service cannot be reduced to nothing more than an efficient operation: its value lies in the less tangible sense that the service is supporting you, meeting your needs, working for and on behalf of you. The real problem with service is that it is still treated as a commodity – as Will Hutton has argued, a commodity 'to be produced at the lowest cost by the most sweated workers'.[7] This mental model of service has a long and deep legacy that colours attitudes in both the commercial and the public sectors.

This legacy began when the first cars rolled off Henry Ford's production line. Although his business was focused on products, his particular model of mass production – the greatest number of goods for the lowest cost and the largest number of people – has become a defining feature of how we see service.

Ford's model had three characteristics that are particularly significant for modern public services. First, costs were lowered through standardising the customer or their needs. Second, it drew a firm line between production and consumption. Goods were created out of the right combination of raw materials, machines and people; these goods were then marketed and sold to the consumers – whose interests and needs had little impact on any activity within the firm. In other words, the value chain was linear, and the recipients of the products were placed firmly at one end of the chain. Third, this separation of production and consumption created demand for managers – professionals whose primary role was to match supply and demand in the most efficient way, and whose positions were defined through access to expert knowledge and insight not otherwise available to the customers.

For a long time, businesses sought to import this manufacturing model of mass production into service provision. More recently, as these organisations discerned a shift in consumer expectations, there has been a greater emphasis on personalised services and products. But when personalisation and manufacturing models collide, a very particular form of personalisation is created. This differentiation is based at best on 'mass customisation' – the breaking down of a particular service or product into modules which customers can then pick and choose from, or add and subtract elements of.

Despite the best efforts of public service innovators up and down the country, our public services continue to be defined by a mass production model. This has created a system that works against professional desires to provide service in the form of support and dialogue to people. Although there are pockets of success around the country in genuinely providing service to people, these successes are more often thanks to professionals circumnavigating the formal system, rather than working with it.

This government has not been blind to the limitations of mass production in creating public services fit for the twenty-first century. Since 1997 their approach to breaking out of this particular model has been guided by an emphasis on the diversification of providers, finding ways of increasing competition and contestability and combining them with central targets and pressure to perform. The almost continuous re-engineering of services that has taken place has been driven in part by a belief that creating a market will bring the consumer values of customer focus, responsiveness and efficiency into a public sector drowning in bureaucracy and paternalism.

But all the evidence suggests that our commercial service experiences are, in general, not much better (and arguably far worse) than our public service experiences. According to research by the National Consumer Council, 81 per cent of people had a bad experience purchasing services last year. Words that came up frequently in relation to commercial service transactions included 'distant', 'clinical' and 'uncaring'.[8] There is no guarantee whatsoever that introducing private providers and market disciplines into the public sector will close the gap between what service organisations do and what it is that people are looking for. There remains a common challenge of service: that large organisations struggle on a daily basis to build genuine and meaningful interactions with their customers and users, and frequently fail to build any kind of responsiveness, flexibility or ability to adapt into their organisational forms.

Why this agenda matters for public service organisations

Commercial service organisations that are unable to connect with their customers risk losing business and profits. However, the risks for public service organisations are far higher. To achieve

the desired outcomes, public services need people to get involved.
The notion of co-production, initially dismissed as jargon that
featured only in the lexicon of aspiring ministers and seasoned
thinktankers, has become part of the new consensus about future
approaches to public service reform. Contrary to Ford's model,
co-production demands that production and consumption are
brought together, so that both can take place simultaneously.
As Sue Goss has argued:

> *Many of the new priorities – 'respect', an end to 'binge drinking',
> 'recycling', 'improved public health' – cannot be achieved by
> a smart government delivery machine; they require changes in
> behaviour from the public. This means not simply reconsidering
> how to deliver using public or even private resources, but how to
> access the 'free' resources of public energy, engagement and action.*[9]

So a child learning is both consuming an education and producing
a cohort of lifelong learners. Someone attending a smoking
cessation course is both consuming a health service and producing
a healthy population. The idea of co-production demands that
public servants and politicians focus not only on the internal
workings and efficiencies of existing services, but also on how
people engage with those services, and how they can be mobilised,
coached and encouraged to participate in the 'common enterprise'
of generating positive outcomes.

In many ways the concept of co-production is not new: our
children are not the first generation of students who need to be
engaged in order to learn. More, what has shifted is our
understanding of the role of the state. The 'five giants' of the
postwar welfare state saw the role of the state as being limited
to developing systems that would help to avoid crises such as
destitution, and provide cures and treatments for problems such
as illness and unemployment. There was a powerful sense that
with benefits came duties, built into a stable institutional and
social framework that has now unravelled. In many ways, debates
over the balance between individual responsibilities and state

intervention was the leitmotif of twentieth-century politics, generating huge debates within political parties as well as cutting across party divides.

The current emphasis on influencing the behaviour of individuals and engaging them in the co-production of outcomes could be seen simply as the latest chapter in a very long book. However, it also reflects an unsung triumph of New Labour. Even if they have not succeeded in transforming public services, they *have* succeeded in turning the tide of public opinion away from low taxation. A significant majority of the population now positively expects investment in public services. Politicians owe it to all of us to respond to these expectations, and frame a new story about what public services are for, and why they matter.

The search for a narrative: people, places and service

Despite the government's attempts to engage people in conversations about why public services matter – for example, through 2003's 'Big Conversation' or this year's 'Let's Talk' campaign – it has in practice put managerialism over vision when considering how to improve and transform public service provision. Performance management, targets and public service agreements became the 'levers' – in the rather mechanistic world view of new public management – for improvements. Alongside the regular spending reviews, commissions such as Gershon and Lyons have been set up to consider how to improve operational efficiencies and service processes.[10] 'Driving out bureaucracy', inspections, regulation and audits simultaneously indicated that this government meant business, and that it believed efficiency could be wrought from a combination of digitisation, process re-engineering, back-office rationalisation and restructuring.

But in all the flurry of activity that has characterised the last ten years, we appear to have forgotten that a reform programme designed to improve the existing safety net was never likely to connect to the challenge of meeting the needs of a society in a state of perpetual change. As Peter Taylor-Gooby has argued, 'the rational incentive-based system that has driven New Labour's approach [to public service reform] risks neglecting the relationships that are so very important in forging trust'.[11]

This pamphlet offers some practical tools and insights from the small but growing discipline of service design as a first step towards re-balancing the emphasis that has been placed on managerialism. Service designers do not see service as something that can be reduced to a commodity. They focus on how people actually experience services, in order to understand how large service organisations can create better relationships with their users and customers.

Experiences and relationships are the recurring themes of this pamphlet. In chapter 1 we argue that engaging people in co-production does not happen through consultations, on citizens' juries or at council meetings: it needs to happen *at the point of delivery* and through conversation and dialogue rather than choice alone. Therefore, learning to understand and map how people experience the point of delivery, the interface between a service and their lives, is essential for creating the conditions for co-production. As we discuss, although smart use of data is important, spreadsheets are no substitute for people.

Chapter 2 explores the pivotal position played by professionals in building relationships between people and services, and understanding how people experience services. We argue that two shifts – one in professional identity and one in the shape of the organisational hierarchy – need to take place if service organisations are to take a relational approach to service design.

Chapter 3 looks at how service innovators are learning to understand these experiences through the eyes of many different and equally complex people, and how they can connect such a diversity of need to the design and evaluation of services without resorting to the mass production model of standardisation. It describes how the most successful service organisations are complementing the ways they measure overall service performance with 'experience metrics' to build up a much richer picture of what really matters to people, and therefore where there is room for improvement.

The fiction writer William Gibson once said, 'the future's already here, it's just unevenly spread'.[12] Throughout this pamphlet you will find a handful of 'near future case studies' of the public service innovators up and down the country who are demonstrating the impact of relational approaches to service reform. By starting with experiences at the interface, these case studies demonstrate that relational approaches combine personalisation and efficiency, at the same time as challenging our current understanding of what these terms mean.

Finally, in chapter 4, we set out the main elements of a different approach to reform – led by the service design principles of this pamphlet – as it applies to the whole system of public services, with different changes occurring simultaneously at different levels. In doing this we pose some questions and challenges for politicians and policy-makers working on public service reform in coming years, and make some suggestions about where they might look to learn more about relational approaches to service.

None of these arguments are about throwing away the positive aspects of current approaches to public service management and reform. But engagement and co-production will grow only out of a deeper, richer understanding of how services relate in practice to people's everyday lives. And in learning more about these 'interface spaces', it is possible that we could also uncover the seeds of a renewed sense of legitimacy for public services. People's level of trust in services is far higher when they are asked about their local secondary school rather than the education system as a whole: we trust that which we know. Learning to have more intimate relationships with people and seeing service as support rather than as a commodity may not only generate the outcomes we are looking for, but also offer the route to securing the legitimacy that public services in the twenty-first century so desperately need.

Service stories

In order to improve their UK business, BUPA relies heavily on the concept of the 'end-to-end patient journey'. Every quarter, senior staff at BUPA Hospitals work with a handful of their customers to trace what happens from the moment someone begins to feel unwell – often some time before that person gets in touch with BUPA. As Alison Platt, head of BUPA Hospitals, says:

> Doing this exercise immediately colours how you think you'll treat that person – the language, the anxiety, the bureaucracy.

Having traced this, BUPA then maps its own processes, technology and interventions to the end-to-end journey. Senior staff ask themselves what each interaction looks like, what transactions are possible, what information any patient really needs. Finally, they add a third line – one that looks at behaviours. As Alison says:

> A call isn't just a transaction, we need to ask: 'How do I want to make you feel?'

A tangible change that has emerged from doing this exercise regularly is that customers calling to discuss their hospital visit are now offered a checklist of things that other people in similar situations have asked. This was introduced after BUPA realised that people often didn't know what to ask when the call finished with the question 'is there anything else I can help you with?' Alison, again:

> You have to do as much as possible to manage getting into people's shoes – psychologically, emotionally, physically.

1
Seeing services as people do

Services need to be understood as a journey or a cycle – a series of critical encounters that take place over time and across channels.

The biggest mistake that large organisations can make is to assume that they know what their service users and customers want. The common challenge of service – the emotional distance between the board and its customers, between local authorities and their citizens – is reflected in low levels of trust and satisfaction. People in general do not often believe that their needs are met by large service organisations in either the commercial or the public sector.

If the primary cause of dissatisfaction people have with service organisations is that they feel misunderstood, ignored, and treated as faceless and nameless, then service organisations need to find new ways of getting to know their users, in all their messy complexity.

> *The attitude here at BUPA about customer research used to be like that of the interested spectator – now we use it to drive decisions.*

In recent years, public sector organisations have demonstrated a growing interest in the tools of the marketing and advertising industries in a quest to learn more about how insights about people can be used to improve what public services offer and how they offer it. The service innovators we met dedicate people and teams to worrying about the question of what it is that people need and want. They constantly search for ways of gaining more – and deeper – insights about their customers. They are alive to the fact that these needs, expectations and desires are subject to change over time and across circumstances. And – most importantly – they constantly strive to connect the insights they gather to organisational strategy, product development, communications and priority-setting.

Alongside the focus on contestability and competition, measures of customer satisfaction and the increasing use of segmentation techniques are seen as the routes by which public services can close the gap between what they do and what people want. In this chapter, we begin by exploring the most innovative practice around the use of customer insight. However, the service innovators we spoke to as part of this project recognised that, while vital, customer insight alone will not generate solutions to the common challenge all large-scale service organisations face. People, in all their complexity and unpredictability, can never be reduced to data. In the latter part of this chapter we look at how successful service organisations keep a steady focus on *experiences* – as a means of guarding against the temptation to put people into boxes or reduce them to a spreadsheet.

Knowing your users, part one

Humans are complex beings. Our organisations are constantly trying to catch up. An ongoing commercial research study[13] now segments all 24 million UK households into 11 groups, 61 types and 243 segments. The study describes each household type in terms of its values, patterns of consumption, likely financial situation and where in the country they are likely to live. This level of complexity can easily feel daunting, but if public service organisations are going to close the gap successfully between what they do and who people are, this complexity needs to be explored and engaged with rather than driven out. Responsive, relational models of service must find ways of visualising users and understanding their needs, fears, aspirations and preferences.

Between them, all the local authorities across the country probably hold more data than the commercial study noted here. The question is how these data are being used. There has been a growing interest in segmentation, and in understanding how to turn raw data into useful insight that improves and targets particular forms of service. For example, the London Borough of Hammersmith & Fulham recently cross-referenced detailed census data with information about the use of services in the borough to target services and communications in each neighbourhood. Their Customer First programme has identified seven customer types including 'childfree prosperous young adults renting from private landlords', and 'older people in poorer health with moderate prosperity'.

Some remain cautious about the value of demographic or social class segmentation. Any approach to dividing down large numbers of people into subgroups is limited by the assumption of homogeneity within each segment. Certainly social class is a likely indicator of the types of services someone may or may not use but used alone it provides little information about how to design the experience of that service for that group. The real richness comes from cross-referencing multiple sources of data.

Beyond the basics

The immutable complexity of people needs to be seen as a source of insight for innovation rather than a productivity headache. New approaches to the design of services use segmentations to break down the more complex dimensions of need, belief and behaviour that shape peoples' responses to service. Such models are developed more rapidly through smaller-scale qualitative studies that are designed to inform service re-design and innovation – and indirectly to derive customer-value metrics from which performance can be measured.

Attitudinal segmentation seeks to understand the meaningful distinctions between the values and beliefs of users with respect to a particular service. This type of segmentation might identify subgroups by statements such as, 'I'm fiercely independent and want to be treated so', or 'I've paid for this service – I'm entitled', or 'I don't want to be a bother'.

Behavioural segmentation groups the practical reasons why people are using a service or channel as the basis for understanding what is required. A behavioural segmentation model might group users by statements such as, 'I need help', 'I need some support', 'I need to complain'.

Journey segmentation recognises that there may be many routes to a single destination such as achieving a healthy body weight. As a nation we need to eat less and do more exercise but simply reminding people of the consequences of not doing this is not going to have a huge impact. Services need to be accessible, but the designers of services also need to have understood the breadth of starting points and the complex emotional journeys that people will need to be motivated to embark on.

These responses to the challenge of complexity reveal new insights that go beyond 'what to provide?' and begin to answer 'how to provide?'

Increasingly service providers are using what they know about their users to create segmented service propositions based loosely around customer types but inviting customers to *self-segment* – to choose from a small number of similar offers and channels based on what they think best matches their own needs. The same offer may be packaged in a number of different ways so that it is not about the choice of which service but the choice of which *experience*. The customer takes control of the choice.

Self-segmentation is one response to the realisation that people increasingly defy segmentation and do not like to be told who they are by big organisations. People exhibit what marketers call multiple personas. We can be professionals, parents, pleasure-seekers and

NIMBYs all in the same afternoon. Elderly people are no longer just elderly. Teenagers are no longer a homogenous group all buying the same music and clothes at the same time.

People are constantly shifting – or are shifted – between the segmentation models of different service providers. A bank identifies someone as one type of person and a phone company identifies them as another. Generally this is not a problem: as consumers, people are in control of these relationships and they are not looking for their bank to sell them phones or their phone company to look after their money. It suits people to be seen and treated differently by different providers when each is offering different things.

The frustration begins when an individual wants to be seen as a whole person and the system can view them only as a collection of isolated segmented subgroups across multiple segmentation models. Speaking at Demos, Jim Murphy MP highlighted the difficulty government has in seeing citizens as individuals.[14] As he pointed out, a single mother is viewed as being at least seven different people across government agencies, including a parent, an employee, a road user, a taxpayer and so on.

The limits of the model

In other words, models of segmentation in the private sector do not necessarily translate wholesale to the more complex service systems in the public sector. In fact the focus on *customer segments* disguises the system of relationships that impact on people's experiences and outcomes. Used in isolation, customer segmentation carries the risk of reducing service interactions to a series of one-to-one transactions and reinforcing the 'provider knows best' paradigm. Such use of data and insight works best when used alongside some of the techniques and methodologies outlined in the next section – techniques designed to prevent service designers from reducing real and complex people to statistics or segments, and to keep a constant focus on the lived experience of the user journey. Data and insight will never replace people.

*As systems get larger, management levels increase . . . but the
visibility of the consumer or user is critical. This isn't to do with
focus groups, but real involvement and development. The consumers
need to stay as real individuals, not just statistics.*[15]

Knowing your users, part two

Using customer insight to tailor services – both in terms of what
is offered and how it is offered – does not necessarily shift the
stubborn legacy of mass production services. Using data to tailor
products and services is similar to drawing information out of
users, re-calibrating and responding. The people represented by this
goldmine of data are still kept at arm's length from the operations
and decision-making processes of the organisation. Similarly,
for people working in those organisations, insights turn people
into numbers, making them two-dimensional.

*In the end, your success will depend less on customer segmentation
and more on your ability to describe the needs of your customer with
great vividness.*[16]

Many of the service innovators we spoke to have recognised
the limitations of customer insight models, even at their most
sophisticated. As a result, they have begun to make the long, slow
and difficult journey to the interface themselves. Rather than
sucking data in, they are experimenting with tools and techniques
that take them to the points at which people actually experience
services. Making this journey enables organisations to understand
in much greater richness how people and services relate in practice.

For public services, we believe these tools and techniques are of
particular interest. The desire to empower users and involve them
in co-producing outcomes is now so common it is almost a truism.
Yet, even with the most determined staff and leaders, the legacy
of mass production makes it almost impossible for such service
organisations to escape their own vantage point on services – as
functional institutions and 'episodes' that interrupt people's lives
– to look afresh at what they are doing from the eyes of users.

And it is hard to escape these prisms. The mobile phone company, Orange, knows from experience that 'making the journey [to see services from a customer's eyes] is very hard, as people have a job within an organisation. Their concern is usually with delivering their part of the service, not putting themselves in the position of the user. Experiencing services from a person's viewpoint is very difficult.'

Seeing your services as your users do is not, unfortunately, a route to simplifying the picture, but it enables organisations to see a different kind of complexity, a complexity that sheds new light on how best to prioritise operational, organisational and policy change. For service designers, the building blocks of service are not episodes and institutions. They are the touchpoints, channels, architectures and journeys that describe services from the starting point of the interface. It is those concepts that the following sections explore.

The tangible elements of service: touchpoints

Touchpoints are the people and tangible things that shape the experience of services (see pages 28–29). The interest in touchpoints originally grew out of organisations seeking to reinforce their brand in ways that went well beyond marketing and mass advertising campaigns. In practice, this recognises that as customers of an airline, we are more likely to remember something about the brand from our interactions with cabin staff, for example, than we are from looking at the design work on the tailfin.

> *Everything we do should be characterised by obsessive and uncompromising attention to detail. We know that any journey is made up of many little experiences and that it doesn't take much to turn a happy customer into an unhappy one. We cannot afford this and we must not let this happen.* [17]

Although branding may not be the top priority for many public service organisations, there is a crucial principle here. Touchpoints are the places and spaces where people experience services. The extent to which their 'brand' invites people in or frustrates them determines the extent to which those people are engaged. And the level of dissonance between what an organisation says it cares about (for example, personalisation or user empowerment) and how people experience that organisation lies at the heart of whether or not people trust such services. People become suspicious if experiences do not match the expectations created by rhetoric, customer charters and organisational commitments.

The need to map public service touchpoints and explore the extent to which they support the commitment to personalisation and co-design is illustrated by the comment of one of our interviewees about a recent hospital experience he had:

> You get the feeling they don't want you there, that they think you're the problem . . . they seem to be saying 'my life running this hospital would be so much easier if you weren't here'. . . . My experience is that hospitals perpetuate my anxiety; when I find myself in this system I feel helpless. There is nothing you can do to ease your anxiety. Information provision is appalling – there's no hand-holding. You find yourself asking several dumb-sounding questions to various people behind desks – it seems as though the system somehow requires you to do so.

In this comment, it is possible to identify a whole range of touchpoints – people, desks, information provision, the hospital building itself – that together combine to *disempower* the person needing the service.

The forgotten touchpoint: service environments

Almost all public services have an implicit association with a designed and built environment. Some of the most profound and emotionally charged interactions with public services happen between four walls where furniture, fixtures, fittings and the design of information play a significant role in shaping people's experiences. Yet so often, they are treated as neutral spaces where 'stuff happens'.

In fact, our behaviour is shaped by the environment. Chris Gerry, head of New Line Learning Federation in Kent, told us that 'the kids behave differently in here [the school] to out there and yet the rules aren't written up, they're embedded'.

Intuitively it's impossible to ignore the impact the built environment has on people's sense of self and agency. For example, one student participating in a *Guardian* book about experiences of school[18] commented that 'the basic aspects of the buildings we are taught in do not promote learning, but instead, enhance feelings of negativity'. Spaces are not empty vessels; they are socially constructed and as such can communicate powerful messages about value, the importance of users and the extent to which they can play an active role in service. One of our commercial interviewees commented:

> *People get psychologically managed by rooms and corridors to adopt behaviours that suit the organisations and support its systems – the spaces are not configured to the needs of those people.*

There is unprecedented capital investment going into the re-design of public service environments at the moment, across schools, hospitals and other public buildings. While such high levels of investment are welcome, there will be a return only if the construction of new buildings grows out of a focus on how spaces can be designed to empower users. This is not about re-creating modernised versions of old buildings. We need to turn the focus to how these buildings relate to the services enacted within them, and communicate to people that they are in control.

In turn, this requires that public services considering new builds start with architectures, rather than architecture. This is a term borrowed from the world of web development. It means the complex and dynamic arrangements of objects, dialogues, information, content, processes and navigation that they work with online. By focusing on architectures, service providers start by considering customer behaviour first, and built architecture second.

For example, many shops and leisure venues create a range of personas to imagine the needs and preferences of people using a space. From this they are able to explore how to respond – through the design of the environment – to the various motivations of their

customers. 'Service blueprints' are developed alongside building blueprints. In this way organisations can design environments that are both instructional and inspirational to a diverse group of users.

Greater access through the proliferation of service channels

In the past, the customers of services tended to stick to a single channel. People booked holidays by sitting in front of a desk in a travel agents, they bought bread from a baker and got their milk from the doorstep. Public services have in recent years begun to expand the number of 'ways in'. Andy Carroll, a strategy manager at the Pensions Service, told us that 'we've made a huge investment in moving from a local paper-based organisation to a national contact organisation'. The goal for the Pensions Service is to move away from office-based services, instead supporting people over the phone, or via one of the 2500 outreach workers who are now working to support such a major 'channel migration'.

The story of the Pensions Service is mirrored all over the public sector. To access health support people can attend a medical drop-in centre, go online or call NHS Direct – which now receives 600,000 calls per month – in addition to making an appointment with their general practitioner (GP). This trend is likely to grow: last year, the Cabinet Office published *Transformational Government* where they argued:

> Over the next decade, the principal preferred channels for the delivery of information and transactional services will be the telephone, internet and mobile channels – as well as increasingly important channels within the digital home . . . government will innovate its services to take swift advantage of new technologies as they emerge.[19]

In this proliferation of channels, of 'ways-in' to services, there are two key questions all service organisations need to address. First, how can they understand the different channel needs and preferences of a diverse set of users; and second, how can they understand the different interactions and relationships between different channels. Any attempt to create an 'integrated channel strategy' (as set out in the Budget earlier this year) needs to start with people's experiences and preferences for different channels, rather than efficiencies alone.

Today, it is no longer possible to assume how a user will access and use a service once many channels are available for them to do so. Therefore every channel needs to some degree to accommodate every kind of user and must be joined-up so that users can move easily between them. Orange, for example, uses a single customer account, which enables them to provide a consistent experience regardless of whether customers decide to call up, go online or visit a store on the high street.

This is important because channels are not simply new routes for delivering services. They remain ways of engaging users, of drawing them in, of helping people to look after themselves. Therefore individual channels and the relationships between them need to be mapped onto people's lives. As a member of the *Transformational Government* team told us, 'solutions need to be about services, not IT'.

To make this real, the government is going to need to do more than 'promote responsible channel choice by telling people how much the use of more efficient channels saves, and what that saving could achieve in terms of reinvestment elsewhere in the public services'.[20] Building the functionality of e-government must not distract government or users from the more difficult challenges of improving services. Technology is of course part of this, but it is by no means the only part.

The interaction of different touchpoints: journeys

Greg Nugent from Eurostar told us:

> *Mapping the customer journey brings together services, products and experiences . . . it's the only way you can see how they interact and how the brand adds up to more than the sum of its parts. Doing the journey made people admit where it was going wrong, because they could see it all in front of them.*

Earlier in this chapter we noted that often service experiences are treated as 'episodes' – interruptions to people's everyday lives. By starting with people and asking them to describe their experiences – as BUPA does, in the example that began this chapter – the focus shifts from looking at episodes, to thinking about journeys: how all the touchpoints and channels come together over a period of time and interact with people's lives, needs, interests and attitudes.

When someone enters prison, they are assessed seven times in the first three days – for level of risk, for health, for learning and development and so on. Each of these assessment touchpoints could be perfectly designed; however, for many prisoners it is frustrating to provide the same information time and time again. It serves to disempower them, to leave them as little more than a figure on an assessment sheet. Focusing on individual touchpoints and exploring the extent to which they 'live the brand' of user empowerment is a vital part of a relational approach to public service transformation. However, equally important is the need to understand the interactions *between* different touchpoints and channels. Equally, if the information taken about these different needs is not pulled together by the organisation, how can it ever provide an integrated service to the prisoner?

Services need to be understood as a journey or a cycle – a series of critical encounters that take place over time and across channels. This is key to integrating the organisation of services around their user, and to combining distributed organisational resources to create experiences and outcomes.

The concept of 'service journeys' is familiar to designers. As a technique it was pioneered and trialled extensively in Scandinavia; it has been used to design everything from aeroplane cockpits to financial trading systems and is increasingly being applied to services in the public and private sectors. As a method, it enables people to create a rich picture of how service experiences play out in the context of everyday life. The objective here is not to understand and optimise operational processes but to determine the best experiential journey for the users of a service.

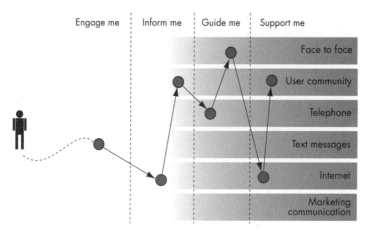

Engage me   Inform me   Guide me   Support me

Face to face

User community

Telephone

Text messages

Internet

Marketing communication

As the example of BUPA demonstrates, mapping a user journey is a far more powerful way of understanding where services could be improved and how engagement could be better encouraged than any kind of large-scale customer satisfaction survey.

But journeys can be used for more than simply identifying problems or points in the service where there is room for improvement. As the users of services are given more choice, and are empowered to make decisions that may previously have been made by experts, it will become more important to include tools to help people manage the uncertainty associated with choice. Talking about 'equipoised choices' in healthcare, Bernard Crump, chief executive of the NHS Institute for Innovation and Improvement argued:

> We need tools to help what need to be sophisticated and paced conversations about decisions to be made – these decisions don't lend themselves well to the seven-minute outpatient model . . . we need to surround that consultation with tools to help people decide what to do.

A service journey is often characterised by a series of choices, which in some instances may have life-changing consequences. Well-designed service journeys should first anticipate and design-out the likely errors that users could make when using services – many of which can be put down to poor information design – and reduce the negative effects of any errors that are made. When possible, service users should be able to *undo* choices and re-choose without incurring penalties. Another strategy to reduce the uncertainty of choosing is to provide the means for users to simulate choices – to play out scenarios and to experiment with the options available. Through the simulation of future journeys the likelihood of making the right choices increases, and the risk and inefficiencies associated with making the wrong choices are reduced.

The new building blocks of service

Insights, segmentation, touchpoints, channels, environments, journeys. It is these, not data, functional institutions and episodes, that constitute the building blocks of services from a user's perspective. If the commitment to creating user-centred services is going to add up to any more than hollow rhetoric, then service organisations need to become experts in the methods, tools and ways of seeing service that ensure they can genuinely make the journey to the interface, and see their services as their users do.

The picture of service is no less complex from the interface as it is from a systemic perspective. What is different, however, is that the interface focuses on how people and services *relate*, not simply the shape of existing services. In tackling the common challenge of service that this pamphlet is focused on, we need to recognise that generating positive outcomes requires engagement, and real engagement comes through experiences. Therefore, being able to map and shape those experiences is the only way that public service organisations will be able to create strategies for genuine improvement and ultimately the transformation of services.

Challenges

* How are you segmenting your users? What combinations of data do you use to create insights?

* Who is responsible for 'user intelligence'? How are they connected to the management of your organisation?

* Are you genuinely looking at your services from the vantage point of the interface?

* Can you map all the touchpoints of your service? Do you know how people feel about these touchpoints?

* How do the different channels of online, phone and face to face interact for different kinds of service users?

* How are you 'designing in' deliberation, dialogue and opportunities for co-creation to the touchpoints and channels of delivery?

A shared language of service

Journeys
Channels
Segmentation
Proposition
Touchpoints
Architectures
Service environments
Personas

Definitions on page 104–106

Y OUR EXPERIENCE MATTERS:

This day, 2006

This newspaper has been designed to be filled in whilst you wait, please don't worry if you can't finish it all as any imput is much appreciated.

EXCLUSIVE NEWS FROM LUTON & DUNSTABLE:

HEAD & NECK PATIENTS TO DESIGN THEIR OWN EXPERIENCE

H neck patients from Luton and Dunstable Head and Neck Clinic asked to get involved with a project to design their own services.

This newspaper has been produced to kick start the consultation process which will include various forms of contact. The core team will be running film workshops where patients will be able to make their own documentary, photography projects among others.

Luton and Dunstable Head and Neck Cancer Services

The multidisciplinary team meeting at the Head and Neck Cancer Clinic starts at 8.30am where some patients' cases are discussed by the team to make decisions on treatment and care. At the same time patients start to arrive at the clinic waiting room. This is an anxious time for patients and sometimes parts of the clinic process heighten that anxiety rather than reduce it. The way the chairs are arranged in the waiting room leaves patients facing a wall full of official notices or looking directly at others; the number of different professionals that seem to be around can be bewildering as are some of the processes. This often leads to a feeling of helplessness, and thinking 'if only the experience could be different':

> You have to get there early to claim a seat otherwise you're standing . . . by the time the consultants arrive at the clinic it is already busy as the clinic shares its waiting area. There are patients and carers standing all over the place, waiting quietly to be seen.

The consulting rooms at the clinic are much like a dentist's; the patient sits in the chair and stares upwards, surrounded by an average of seven members of staff, and it is in this situation that most patients are given their diagnosis.

Across the NHS patients are rarely involved in healthcare improvement beyond mechanisms such as focus groups and questionnaires. Luton and Dunstable Hospital Head and Neck Cancer Services has been taking an innovative approach to the ongoing re-design of their service, which is putting patients and staff right at the centre of the process.

The project has been sponsored and supported by the NHS Institute for Innovation and Improvement and is co-produced with the service design consultancy, thinkpublic, anthropological researchers from University College London and, importantly, patients and staff from the hospital. The objective has been not to solve any specific problem of service delivery, but to achieve an improved experience of the service by involving staff and patients in the process of re-design. To do this, a range of techniques has been used to help patients and staff describe their experiences with a specific focus on the touchpoints.

A project team was brought together that comprised patients, carers, healthcare staff, researchers and improvement leaders. The core project team knew that the initial engagement with patient carers and staff would be critical, so in the build-up to the project they engaged with their audience through a range of communication media including posters, leaflets and a low-tech newspaper to create interest. Patients and staff were invited to become involved in examining the service in ways that were unfamiliar to most of them.

A participatory design project like the one at Luton and Dunstable is not something that staff can be coerced or targeted to get involved in. Vital to its success is that those who take part are willing and energised participants. As a subtle mechanism of recruitment onto the project, all staff were invited to keep log books and to note their own thoughts, frustrations and ideas about the service they were providing. Deborah Szebeko, a member of the service design team, told us:

> We had a strong sense that patients wanted to get involved because they felt that they wanted to give something back to the service. Staff were excited to work with patients in a way that was different from their usual relationship with patients.

Insight was generated in a number of ways including further work with the log books and patient interviews. The patients and staff mapped a set of touchpoints that they felt formed their experience of Head and Neck Cancer Services and re-played their emotional journeys through the service. These touchpoints then formed the key focus for re-design. Many of the touchpoints that were identified can be re-designed very easily and would make a huge difference to the patient experience. For example, staff moved weighing scales out of sight of the waiting room – they hadn't noticed how embarrassing patients found it to be weighed in front of everyone.

Film was also used as a way to encourage involvement – literally handing over the lens through which the service was viewed to patients and bringing their lived experiences to life for others. Patients found this process to be an incredibly powerful way to share their stories and be heard. When patient's films were shown during working sessions it immediately created a shared understanding and a new empathy for the deeper needs of patients. The effect was to connect and energise the group towards a common purpose – to improve the patient, carer and staff experience. As Deborah told us:

> While we did have some concerns that re-living and sharing these types of experiences might be difficult for patients, the majority felt that it was invaluable in helping them to move forward and in building relationships with other patients, carers and staff.

Many patients suggested that the project methodology of filmmaking that they had been invited to work on should become part of the patient journey itself – an example of how handing control over to users in the context of a designed methodology becomes an aspect of service in its own right:

> We've had one patient working closely with us and visiting our studio to edit his film; he has helped bridge a gap and get staff on board with film. He is extremely passionate and just really wanted to help; he has taken time off work to get involved with the project. He also feels he is learning new skills.

In this example, service design, service delivery and insight generation happen simultaneously and collaboratively at the interface. As one patient of the service said:

> *I enjoyed meeting everyone – feeling I was eating properly for the first time, possibly because I was in company.*

This type of participatory design intervention led the team to conclude that the principle of building continuous service improvement mechanisms into the everyday experience for both patients and staff – rather than being an independent activity – can add an incredible amount of value to the service. And importantly, it helps to improve communication between patients and those staff who are providing care.

Through mapping user journeys, patients articulated clearly that this clinic represented a 'pinprick' in comparison to their whole journey, which involved many other departments and hospitals – as well as touchpoints outside of the formal system. This demonstrates the wider challenge for health services in working together across the whole patient journey.

The process so far has opened up a new dialogue between staff and patients. The project – which now has its own active blog – has connected people with the same interest in improving the touchpoints of the service and has given 'permission' and a structure to make small but significant changes happen. Lynne Mahar at the NHS Institute for Innovation and Improvement commented: 'The process so far has challenged traditional views and experiences of service improvement, giving patients and staff a new energy and commitment for change.' Together they are trialling how the clinic's space is used; instead of the consultants having rooms, which patients move in and out of, patients now have rooms and staff move to see them. The clinic is now building a closer relationship with neighbouring Mount Vernon Hospital, which provides radiotherapy, to build a better understanding of the wider patient experience.

The project is still work in progress but staff appear to be more motivated to work with patients. Patients are calling staff to arrange times to meet; they appear to be mobilised and active in co-designing and trialling ideas. The perceived risk expressed by some staff that involving patients in this way would unfairly raise their expectations and lead to disappointment has not transpired. As one member of the team pointed out:

> Patients and staff are not asking for gold taps, in fact most of their suggestions are quite achievable with a little budget. I would say one of the most important things is providing space for relationships to build and supporting that with communication.

The experience of connecting patients and staff in this way has proved to be extremely valuable in changing beliefs about what they can achieve. This combination of experience and belief has led to positive action, resulting in change that will actually improve experiences.

Service stories

Peter Gilroy, now chief executive of Kent County Council, told us that 'the quality of interactions is my obsession . . . relationships are the glue that hold everything together'. In his previous job, as strategic director of Kent Social Services, his first step towards achieving 3-star status was to work on improving the experiences of his staff working at the council: 'If we can't look after our staff, they are not going to look after our customers.' He produced a ten-point plan that focused on two dimensions: people's work 'on the job' and their quality of life overall. Training and career progression was a major focus, as was work–life balance and staff health. But Peter's approach went beyond simply making life better for his frontline professionals: he took that focus and used it to demand that people re-imagined the shape of the organisation:

> I wanted to create a paradigm shift to show that the front of our business was more important . . . you've got to take very seriously the behavioural and care aspects of the workforce – and I don't mean of your senior people, your priority must be the front of the business . . . transformation isn't just about things, it's about behaviours and mindsets.

High expectations are rewarded with recognition and validation for good work. Kent has regular 'Oscar' ceremonies for frontline staff, and employees from any area of the council can qualify for exchange trips around the world if they have performed excellently. Under Peter's leadership, Social Services reached 3-star status and Kent is now one of four 4-star councils – suggesting that his determination to put the frontline centre stage reaps powerful benefits not only for the people working there but also for the citizens of Kent.

2
Professionals and practitioners

Find ways of enabling professionals and people to work together: create spaces for simultaneous empowerment.

Richard Elliot, former manager of a drugs action team in Bristol, found himself dealing with a tangle of 44 different funding streams, nine planning grids and 82 different objectives. By his estimation, he and his team spent little more than 40 per cent of their time actually working to tackle drug issues. Unsurprisingly he resigned, writing that 'monitoring has become almost religious in status, as has centralised control . . . the demand for quick hits and early wins is driven by a central desire analogous to the instant gratification demands made by drug users themselves'.[21]

Richard's story is echoed in a wider complaint about the impact of targets of professional autonomy and identity. Public service professionals and practitioners are growing increasingly vocal about the unintended consequences of targets, arguing that their cumulative impact adds up to disengaging, frustrating and alienating experiences for service users. Practitioners recognise that many people approach a service organisation and are made to jump through a set of complicated hoops in order to meet an apparently straightforward request. The agents they are interacting with are not doing what seems obvious to meet the request, because they are instead driven to focus on doing whatever they need to do in order to meet the target. Those who work at the frontline of public services argue that this runs entirely counter to why they took their jobs in the first place, and that targets from central government undermine their professional autonomy. Their frustrations stem in the main from the sense that the system prevents them from providing the support they want to give as professionals.

But this is not a straightforward story about 'oppression by target'. At the start of this pamphlet we described the notion of mass production services, a model where one of the most distinctive features is a particular form of professional identity. This identity is characterised by access to expert knowledge and insight not otherwise available to people and users: the primary job of the professional is to match supply and demand in the most efficient way through acting as gatekeepers to services. The impact of this on people's experiences of services is just as profound as the target culture about which professionals complain: such models of professionalism create an unequal distribution of power. Sitting in the consulting room as a patient is a very different experience from sitting in that same room as the doctor.

Over the years organisations have tried to improve the quality of interactions between staff and customers through introducing behaviour guides – such as requiring staff to look customers in the eye, wishing them a good day with a pleasant smile. These are all important, but only if they stem from a deeper, more profound shift in how staff and customers understand their relationship. In this chapter we explore the place of people-facing professionals in organisations that are innovating services. Drawing on our case study organisations we argue that two themes need to be put at the heart of approaches to reform. The first is the task of shifting notions of professional identity from being about expertise and knowledge to being about building capacity to cope. The second is to 'design in' a focus on the frontline, the interface space between people and services.

The zero-sum game of professional and public autonomy

Ninety-one per cent of people with long-term health conditions report a desire for a greater say in decisions about their treatment.[22] Every week, 52 million Americans go online to find out about health.[23] Parents overwhelmingly see other parents, not professionals such as health visitors and parent practitioners, as the experts.[24] In searching for meaning and recognition, people are looking for greater autonomy and an understanding that they want the right to make decisions about their own lives, as the people who best know the social, cultural and economic context of such decisions.

The rhetoric of user-led public services put forward by this government risks polarising professional and user empowerment as if it were a zero-sum game. For example, in autumn 2005, the Prime Minister made a speech in which he argued that 'public service reforms [in health and education] must be driven by the wishes of the users not the producers'.[25] There is a sense that if users need to be put at the heart of public services, then providers, producers, departments, agencies and councils must step back, cede power and stop pursuing their own interests and preferences.

Yet advocating user empowerment in this way will not resolve the tension that characterises debates about the place of people-facing professionals in public services. Relational public services require dialogue, empathy and understanding. Over 30 years ago, Ivan Illich wrote passionately about the need to go beyond existing models of professional–user relationships. In *Deschooling Society* he argued that 'good institutions encourage self-assembly, re-use and repair. They do not just serve people but create capabilities in people, support initiative rather than supplant it'.[26] Far from seeking to set user interests and producer interests at odds, future approaches to reform need to focus on how people and service staff can work together to create outcomes.

When Richard Duvall founded the online bank Egg, he set out to create a bank that could 'dance with its customers' – a bank that could respond to changing needs, expectations and preferences. Similarly, the most successful service organisations are finding ways of recognising people's professionalism through being experts in designing support collaboratively with people. Professional expertise continues to exist, but it is deployed differently: rather than solving problems or telling people what to do, this expertise is used to uncover needs and help people navigate a complex network of possible support.

The professional as expert but not as we know it

The collective good is made up of millions of different, sometimes intimate decisions and experiences about the way people lead their lives. These decisions depend on relationships – more or less equal, more or less deep, more or less extended, but always a two-way exchange between public and professional.[27]

The tension – that on the one hand, professionals feel disempowered by targets, and on the other, dominant models of professional identity keep the power on the side of the service organisations, not the users, will not be resolved through setting staff and users against one another. The challenge, instead, is to focus on how professionals and people can *work together* to create outcomes. Service innovators have focused on creating spaces where professional and personal autonomy can grow simultaneously. They have done this through fostering a form of professional identity, vested less in expert knowledge and more in capabilities to provide deep support to individuals, to motivate them to help themselves. As Charles Leadbeater has argued, 'professionals should serve people in a way that builds up distributed capacity for coping.'[28]

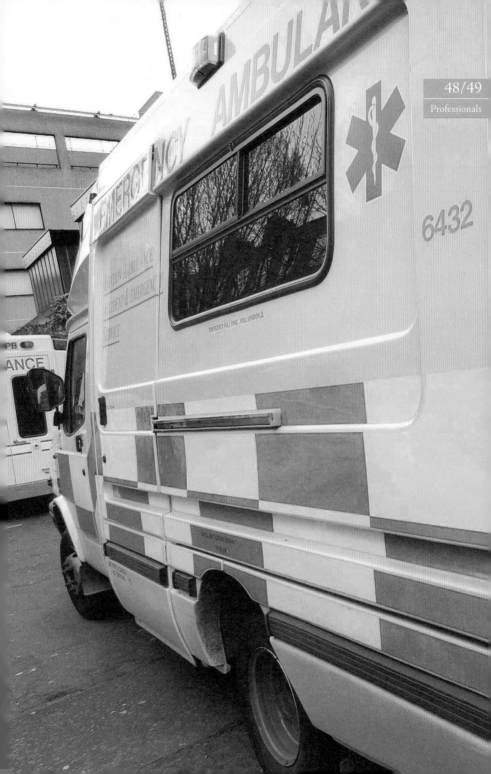

If outcomes are more likely to be achieved when reform to public services starts with the experiences and interfaces between people and services, it is clear that frontline workers are an essential part of the jigsaw puzzle. Despite expanding options for 'self-service', many of the most complex problems people face go beyond the boundaries of DIY service. However, the insights put forward in this chapter apply just as much to the fleeting interactions between people and service professionals as they do to longer-term relationships. Relational approaches to reform are not all about forming long-term relationships over time; instead they are about a set of qualities – empathy, recognition and understanding – and a consequent focus on dialogue. As one participant from a local authority said to us: 'We aspire to create relationships with our customers but at the moment we barely give them a one night stand. What's important isn't the length of the relationship but the extent to which I feel understood and listened to *at that moment*.'

Putting the frontline centre stage

Chapter 1 has already described how hard it can be for large organisations to genuinely see their services from their users' perspectives. Equally, making the case for empowering staff to work collaboratively with users is far easier than creating organisations where all the surrounding systems and processes align with those professional values and expectations. A common theme in all the organisations we met is that an unerring focus on creating highly satisfying customer experiences has to be sponsored from the top. Similarly, such a focus can sometimes lead to short-term losses in order to make long-term gains. For example, in 2005, BUPA processed £90 million of ineligible claims. It did so because its frontline staff had worked with the customers and decided that, for whatever reason, there was a good case to process the claim. By doing this, BUPA is effectively communicating to its staff that listening to the customer is more important than enforcing the rule book. Customer satisfaction and loyalty, rather than immediate profit, is an important part of BUPA's long-term commercial position and the management communicates this effectively to staff and customers alike when it goes ahead and deals with those ineligible claims.

The remainder of this chapter outlines how successful service organisations have taken a simple principle – that professionalism needs to be rooted in empathy, support and dialogue – and threaded it through every layer of their business, from individual accountability, to shared values, to organisational systems, benefits and processes. It is this 'Russian doll' approach that ensures that this is about far more than simply overlaying old models of service with new indicators of customer service. Instead these organisations demand a lot from their people-facing professionals; but in return they put the frontline – the interface – centre stage and shape the organisation around the pursuit of high-quality interactions between people and services.

Accountability for experiences: defining professionalism for individuals
Recruiting for empathy

first direct, judged to be the number one bank in terms of customer service, explicitly hires 'empathetic people' – and interestingly, many former nurses and teachers can be found on the payroll. John Lewis Partnership speaks of the importance of recruiting partners who are experts – but as Patrick Lewis, their supply chain manager pointed out, 'we need to be careful that people are experts in customers not products'. They recruit predominantly on attitude rather than experience; this is reflected not only in how they bring in new recruits, but also by the fact that many of their senior positions are filled through internal promotions.

Large organisations need to find new ways, not only of encouraging, but of making inevitable a focus on the extent to which staff respond to and support people seeking service. The dialogue and conversation that sits at the heart of relational approaches is about more than listening. It requires staff to be empathetic, to have an 'intuitive unity' with people that is driven by their recognition of the emotional, social and cultural context of service experiences.

Guardians of the customer experience

Many of the organisations we met over the course of this research had introduced performance frameworks that evaluated every member of staff on the basis of their contribution to positive customer experiences, in addition to some other more traditional measures of job performance.

For example, at Virgin Atlantic staff are appraised on the extent to which they perform as guardians of the customer experience. Angus Struthers told us:

> Staff have to remember that they are not just working for Virgin Atlantic, but they're working for the passenger and they have got to be able to put themselves in the shoes of the passenger, and ensure that passengers receive the kind of experience they would like to receive, as corny as that may sound.

And as Alex Popple at MSN UK said:

> We're incentivised around doing things that are ground-breaking ... everybody is supposed to have an objective around improving the customer experience.

Open and shared professional values and behaviours

The most successful service organisations have understood that they cannot simply legislate for how staff relate to customers through performance frameworks. These organisations have also focused on how to keep relational values alive, to stop them from ossifying in company mission statements or job descriptions that get buried in human resources folders. They are experimenting with new ways of distributing capacity for holding staff to account on responding to people's needs. They are permanently looking for new ways of fostering a sense of mutual accountability.

BUPA and Tesco have invested considerable company time in working with staff to develop the values that guide relationships with customers. For example, at BUPA Hospitals, the senior management team worked with all staff to answer the question:

'If you were doing your job brilliantly, what would it look like?' Significant organisational time was put aside to consider the question. The result is not a fixed set of job descriptions, but rather a series of excellence profiles for all staff, ranging from catering managers to consultants, that represent a shared set of values to which people can be held to account. Everyone is able to access any excellence profile they wish through a central system. Rather than defining a specific set of activities, the profiles are aspirational and are firmly grounded in the organisation's mission to 'take care of the lives in our hands'.

Similarly, about five years ago, Tesco held a series of day-long seminars for literally thousands of staff. The purpose of these sessions was to start a conversation about what Tesco stood for, and what it should stand for. The results were boiled down into two simple, memorable lists: 'four things we do for customers' and 'six things we do for each other'. In developing these lists, Tesco successfully created a shared agenda, used and owned by staff up and down the country.

Pret a Manger uses its recruiting process to remind staff of its values and encourage them to own them. Every applicant who wants to work at Pret is invited to an 'experience day' – a day where they go and work in the store to which they have applied. At the end of the day, the rest of the staff vote on whether or not the applicant met the criteria of customer focus that all Pret employees are held to account on. If fewer than 90 per cent of staff believe that this is the case, then the person does not get offered the job.

Experiences at the interface drive organisational priorities too

The story of Peter Gilroy's ten-point staff plan outlined at the start of this chapter illustrates another common theme from the organisations we spoke to over the course of this research. All had high expectations of staff. But they also tried to provide a lot in return, both in terms of recognition and support. As Peter Simpson, former commercial director at first direct, said, 'people are people –

the only difference between a person working here and a person not working here is that we're paying one of them'.

Another important characteristic of these organisations is that they sought to learn from their staff – about how organisational systems and processes stood in the way of being able to provide support, or about which rules worked against positive experiences between services and people. Good service organisations treat their staff as the 'eyes and ears', able to advocate powerfully for how things can be improved for users or customers.

Training and celebrating

The organisations we spoke to spent disproportionate amounts of time and money on supporting staff to achieve more. For example, Pret spends virtually nothing on advertising. Instead, they take the 6–7 per cent revenue that would normally be spent on marketing activities, and reinvest it in training and fun. Pret staff are offered free English lessons and regular parties. For Pret, as with many other good service organisations, they do not believe it is possible to ask staff to focus on empathy and relationships with customers without building in a people-centric culture to the organisation itself.

Similarly, Peter Gilroy in Kent fought hard to invest 2 per cent gross every year on training and research – despite widespread concerns about deficits. He remained firm, however, arguing that such investments always bring better returns. He backed up this investment by insisting on regular celebrations of and rewards for staff success. The awards celebrations they hold, which senior staff are expected to attend, celebrate staff who have been judged excellent by users. High-performing teams and individuals are rewarded by funding for study trips around the world. As Peter argued, the total cost of these activities adds up to little more than a single national advertisement for a new post, and yet they are key to empowering, enthusing and ultimately retaining his staff, who he regards as his most valuable asset. In his words, the training and mentoring schemes, as well as the parties, became 'part of the ether, part of the gold dust' that have contributed to the organisation improving its services so successfully in recent years.

Such anecdotal evidence about the impact of training is supported by larger-scale studies. Bassi Investments charted the performance of a share portfolio of companies with high investments in training over five years, against the 'Standard & Poor's 500' (a US equivalent of the FTSE 100). The findings were clear: the US firms that made the largest investments in employee skills made the largest returns (16.3 per cent per annum) compared with the average return (10.7 per cent) across the index. In other words, investors received a 52 per cent higher return over five years from shares in companies that make high investments in training.[29]

Quality of work

Professionals should be paid fairly for their work, but not at the expense of the working conditions themselves. Increasingly, we are recognising that control over working time and conditions, self-management and forms of democratic control over the workplace are as important as the traditional trade union agenda of pay and conditions. Research in the UK has found, for example, that autonomy ranks higher than hours and pay as a factor in determining job satisfaction.[30]

Building lateral capacity

Ask most people-facing staff who they could learn from most and the response will usually be other people doing their jobs elsewhere. For too long, public service workers have been trapped within their own zones of practice – whether that's the classroom, the district or the GP's surgery. The continuous process of professionals learning how to respond, and taking on a mantle of 'solutions-assemblers' or 'advocates' as part of the shift in professional identity described above (see page 48), can be sped up and supported by a focus on fostering lateral connections through the development of communities of practice or 'action learning groups'.

Organisations that seek to facilitate and support such lateral networks are effectively communicating to their staff that they recognise that knowledge, ideas and expertise are not located in the central office, but instead at the frontline. In spelling out and backing up this message, organisations can demonstrate their support for staff from whom they are demanding high levels of empathy and entrepreneurialism in meeting people's needs. One respondent said to us: 'Organisations need to give people mirrors to compare themselves to others. This is the only way you'll overcome the temptation of command and control.'

There are two further benefits to fostering peer networks of people-facing staff. First, innovation no longer happens in isolation, but instead through teams. Encouraging people to work together and experiment with fresh approaches to meeting people's needs can increase staff satisfaction and create more positive service experiences. Second, finding ways of sharing knowledge can create efficiencies and prevent people from inventing the same wheel many times over.

Learning from people-facing professionals

Our success is built on insights from individuals on the frontline.

Chapter 1 discussed the importance of opening out the channels by which data and insight can be used to drive organisational priorities and development. Alongside gathering insights from users and customers directly, the service organisations we spoke to created the time, space and expectation that staff insights would also drive the process of priority-setting and problem-solving for the organisation.

For example, John Lewis Partnership holds weekly 'consultation half-hours' where staff are able to share insights about what's working well and what is working less well in each of the stores. These are discussed at the individual store level as well as at the national office. Last month, Peter Gilroy sent out a message via payslips to all his employees, asking them each to 'take five' – to think for five minutes about new ways that Kent could generate income for its work.

Insights about service improvements are valuable by-products of interactions between professionals and users, and organisations need to ensure that they develop the mechanisms and channels that are able to capture and use these insights. Just as setting up communities of practice underlines to staff that they are the ones likely to have the best ideas, creating these opportunities for feedback – and demonstrating that this feedback can have an impact on strategy – is a crucial part of creating a culture that puts activity at the interface centre stage.

Relational approaches to service put frontline professionals at the centre stage, alongside users, as key characters at the interface between people and services. This has implications both for the professionals themselves and for the way in which the frontline is connected to the rest of the organisation. For the successful service organisations that feature in this report, professionals – their roles and identities – play a crucial role in focusing on experiences and engaging people. The challenge, in their terms, is to create the space and capacity for people and professionals to grow their autonomy simultaneously – and to shape an organisation that actively supports this.

Challenges

- ✦ What are the key aspects of professional identity in your organisation?

- ✦ Do your job descriptions, recruitment strategies and performance frameworks reflect a firm commitment to improving user experiences of service?

- ✦ How have you invested in training and recognition for your staff?

- ✦ How are you connecting frontline professionals to each other?

- ✦ What are the natural points of common interest and social contact?

- ✦ Which aspects of organisational routine offer opportunities for garnering staff feedback?

- ✦ What connections to organisational structure and strategy need to be made in order for staff ideas to flow into corporate priorities?

- ✦ Where does your organisation learn its collective lessons?

A shared language of service

Guardians of the customer experience
Mutual accountability
Excellence profiles
Communities of practice

Definitions on pages 106–107

Birmingham OwnHealth

Pfizer Health Solutions is working with NHS Direct and two primary care trusts (PCTs) in Birmingham to create an innovative approach to service. Launched earlier this year, Birmingham OwnHealth will support up to 2000 people with diabetes, heart failure and/or cardiovascular disease. It draws on health prevention models used in the USA where the focus is less on efficiency of existing services, and more on changing projections and trends. John Procter, who leads the Pfizer Health Solutions team working on the scheme, argues that there is a need to invest in the value of health, and move beyond simply looking at the costs. He sees the work in Birmingham as an opportunity to demonstrate what this looks like in practice:

> Innovative partnerships such as this one can play a crucial role in helping the NHS shift from being a 'sick' care system towards being a patient-centred 'health' care system. It will deliver benefits to all – individuals and their families, clinicians and healthcare professionals, and the wider NHS.

At the heart of Birmingham OwnHealth is the ambition to reduce the number of 'non-scheduled' visits to secondary care – by far the most expensive element of health services – through enabling people to better manage their conditions and prevent them from escalating:

> Programmes like this don't save money immediately – but they do reduce the growth of trends over time . . . it's as much about what you don't spend as what you do.

Birmingham OwnHealth has innovated in terms of the channel they use: it is a service delivered entirely over the telephone, on the basis that phones are in people's homes and part of their everyday lives, even if they are not very mobile. To make the service as accessible as possible, it is offered in two languages (English and Punjabi) and all supporting patient information has two versions – one for high literacy and one for low literacy.

The scheme's success also rests on how the frontline professionals are trained: the focus is on their professional role and interactions with the patient and the need to build relationships with the people they are supporting and the surrounding services that each patient may wish to access. Rather than using their clinical expertise to instruct people, the NHS Direct nurses are trained to use that expertise to guide people to reach their own conclusions instead:

> It's totally different to an inbound system that uses algorithms . . . it's about coaching and support and conversation.

This alternative model of professionalism is supported by the design of the scheme's knowledge management and needs assessment system – a digital platform developed by Pfizer Health Solutions. In the first conversation, the care manager will ask some simple questions – for example about diet, exercise and so on – and the system will highlight areas where the patient needs to do some work. Together, the care manager and the patient will talk in order to understand which issues are relatively straightforward to tackle, and those where the patient feels they need more support to tackle. They then set some targets – not based on system performance but instead on the goals that the patient feels they can achieve through the conversations and coaching offered by the nurses. The ultimate goal is for each individual to begin to have a positive impact on their health and wellbeing through taking action built on the confidence, knowledge and understanding they have gained through working with their care manager. In time people will eventually graduate from the programme, with the 'graduation criteria' being focused on capacity to self-manage, rather than a pre-defined set of outcomes that may mean different things to different individuals.

Birmingham OwnHealth has also begun to knit together the whole range of local services for their users. They are mapping what they call the 'local service ecology' – noting the locations for specific services to help guide users towards what they are looking for. In time this map will help the PCT in collaboration with GP surgeries to ensure that services are evenly distributed. Staff work with people from specific GP surgeries to enable them to build up relationships and provide regular feedback on the patients on the scheme to help ensure continuity across different service channels.

John talks about how hard it can be to measure the impact of their work, particularly for the handful of patients at risk of developing cardiovascular disease who are not yet suffering but are highly likely to have an 'incident' in the next ten years. Using Prochaska's model of behaviour change,[31] he says, 'moving someone from pre-contemplation to contemplation to action over the course of the year or more may represent real progress towards prevention, but there's nothing in it that can be reflected on a balance sheet'. Yet, as he rightly points out, the savings generated by reducing the impact from these kinds of diseases, even by 1 per cent, are far higher than any figure saved through rationalising existing services.

It's early days yet for the scheme but John tells us that local staff in the PCT are already excited:

> Birmingham OwnHealth is not about replacing services at a local level, it's about enhancing and improving what's already there. We've learnt that you should just start somewhere, anywhere, and let the rest of it grow and develop over time . . . it's the hardest thing to get started, but once you have it's possible to see what else could grow from it.

3
Measuring success

Find ways of measuring experiences as well as systems: life is more complicated than a key performance indicator.

Seeing service as a delivery mechanism rather than a transformative experience has led to a particular form of information gathering and system measurement. Existing targets have tended to focus energy on underperformance in operational efficiency, at the expense of underperformance in the transformation of people's lives. Being able to assess the quality of the experience is as important as knowing the efficiency of the operations: both are necessary forms of measurement. As Patrick Lewis from John Lewis Partnership told us, 'you've got to run the organisation at a more complex level than that of KPIs'.

Chapter 1 explored the sorts of insights successful organisations gather from their customers and users. The insights these organisations seek to collect go beyond demographics and even attitudes – they are also interested in what people think about something, how they felt about a particular experience or product. What this reveals, therefore, is that by gathering information about customers and what matters to them, service organisations also begin to gather a form of *feedback*, which itself provides measures of success. Rather than this success being measured at a systemic level (such as progress against targets), such insights represent the measurement of success from an *experiential* perspective – from the vantage point of the user themselves on the service they are accessing. This matters because, when it works, users themselves experience success directly, with obvious consequences for their sense of satisfaction and trust.

In other words, successful service organisations have found ways of measuring success and improvement at *more* than the systemic level. The information flow between users and the organisation is far more dynamic, and customer insights are treated as a form of measurement for assessing performance *at the same time* as determining priorities. The service innovators we spoke to understand that unless they can see what is working and what is going wrong from the perspective of the user, they have little hope in engaging that person, or (in the case of commercial organisations) keeping their custom.

Measuring impact and success by experience metrics can be revealing. Take, for example, the civil justice system. In recent research for the Department for Constitutional Affairs, as many as a third of people felt that the experience of sorting out the issue was at least as stressful as the issue itself. A further third felt that both were equally stressful. And the knock-on effect of these experiences on other issues that relate to other public service provision is telling as well: respondents highlighted illness, as well as employment and relationship issues as side effects of their problems and the experiences of trying to resolve them.[32]

Don't let a key performance indicator get in the way of doing what's right: measuring experiences

There are tensions between the need to look at a single customer view and the overview. We need to do both. The two together can be very revealing, and can expose deep structural problems.

Not only do measures of experience add a richness to existing approaches to system measurement, in some cases they illuminate the unintended consequences of targets and efficiency metrics. A number of people we interviewed as part of this project spoke of the detrimental impact system measures can have on people's experiences of service, and warned against placing too much value on a 'single view' of performance information. For example, one representative of John Lewis Partnership said to us that he 'doesn't let a KPI stand in the way of doing what's right'. This was supported by the views of many of the local authority representatives we spoke to. As one respondent said:

> The problem is the monitoring. Targets are increasingly driving provision. Councils are now learning sophisticated ways of 'playing the game', pouring resources into those things on the boundaries of target levels. This distorts the relationship with customers.

The actual experiences of people, rather than the detached measurements of customer satisfaction and proxy measures of performance such as waiting times, should be used as drivers for service transformation. The trick is to measure performance in ways that illuminate the quality of the experience rather than focusing solely on operational performance. Organisations need to measure what users value, as well as what organisations and service systems value.

The public sector has already begun to adopt many of the customer research techniques that are used in the private sector. Focus groups are used to test ideas and support service planning. Some service providers are commissioning mystery shopping research to directly assess the quality of customer service. Pret's mystery shoppers assess not only the range of products on offer, but also the quality of service. They have turned apparently soft measures of human interaction into harder metrics: did the barista look you in the eye and smile? Did they tell you how much change you were receiving?

The government has until recently advocated a unified cross-service measure of customer satisfaction as a means of adding experiential measures to the system metrics already in place. However, the problem with satisfaction as a measure is that it is highly subjective if viewed from the perspective of the users. People bring different expectations – often shaped by their own circumstances and backgrounds – to service experiences; all satisfaction measures is the extent of the gap between those expectations and perceptions. Expectations and perceptions are highly individual and changeable.

So, more needs to be done to identify ways of measuring actual service experiences. The service organisations we spoke to are pioneering a number of experience metrics, all of which could be applied to public service organisations as a way of enriching the means by which system performance is understood.

Tesco has developed a management and measurement tool that they call the Steering Wheel. The wheel is based on the theory of the balanced scorecard that prompts businesses to consider not only the financial performance, but the impact on the bottom line of the happiness of employees, the efficiency of operations and the satisfaction of customers. Tesco has five customer-value metrics derived from customer research – a notably small number – that they believe are the five aspects of the supermarket experience that are most important to customers: the aisles are clear, I can get what I want, the prices are good, I don't want to queue, the staff are great. Tesco believes that things need to be simple if they are to be applied at every level of the organisation, from boardroom to stockroom.

Alex Cheatle from TEN UK, a lifestyle management and concierge business, explained:

> We measure ourselves based on what they [our clients] want. We ask each member, exactly what/when/how do you want? and our system then tracks everything we do against that expectation, using time tracking and feedback loops. We haven't come across a single call centre that can deal with this level of complexity.

This form of measurement – in customer terms, not universal standards set centrally and sometimes arbitrarily based on what users might judge to be good – can be called my-metrics. My-metrics are also an important part of Birmingham OwnHealth, the case study described at the end of chapter 2.

Paul Bello from Orange described the current high point of success measures in the commercial sector as the *propensity to recommend*. 'Would you recommend this service to someone else?' has become the only question worth asking customers for some organisations in assessing success. The theory is that most customer surveys are inherently inaccurate as questions can be asked in ways that lead to positive responses. But ask people if they would recommend a plumber, for example, and they are forced to put their own reputation on the line.[33]

The current approach to inspecting schools and hospitals at periodic intervals is one of the most stressful elements of any public service manager's job. Staff sickness increases in schools around the time of Ofsted inspections as school staff feel under tremendous pressure to perform against the criteria set by the system. Chris Gerry, head of New Line Learning Federation in Kent, might therefore be regarded as a glutton for punishment in deciding to invite Ofsted in on a much more regular basis. He supplements their inspections with his own feedback system. Every month students are asked to provide feedback on teacher performance against a number of metrics that the students themselves were involved in devising. These metrics are focused on things like whether the lessons were boring or engaging, whether homework was marked on time, and so on, rather than student grades. As Chris puts it, 'we know that the best way of creating lifelong learners is to engage them', so measuring the success or otherwise of this engagement is crucial.

What Chris is doing is measuring service experiences *as they unfold*. Not only does this provide him with a much more constant flow of information and feedback that enables him to pinpoint in more detail where work is needed, it also reduces the levels of stress associated with measuring success. Feedback is not used to punish people; it is used to prioritise the activity of Chris and his senior colleagues. It creates an atmosphere of continuous improvement. Furthermore it makes small-scale experimentation and innovation less risky: teachers at Chris's school can get almost immediate feedback on the impact of any changes they make to their teaching practice – all the data is available for everyone to see and use.

Feedback, measurement and information at the interface
Closing the gap between the interface and the boardroom
User insights can be challenging, demanding and uncomfortable for organisations. However, the most innovative service organisations see beyond this. They view their service users as a resource or specialist network to draw on for development ideas. For example, BUPA seeks out the things that are not working about its service. As Alison Platt, head of BUPA Hospitals said, 'the challenge is always to get people to believe that the service on offer can be improved'. As well as investing significant time and money in following user journeys and evaluating how touchpoints and channels can be improved, BUPA's customer intelligence team focuses on the four elements of BUPA's service that customers like least. These are identified through focus groups and customers are then invited to work with senior management to make a plan of action to tackle these issues. Progress is assessed and fed back. What is significant is the dynamic nature of the flow of information through BUPA. This process is repeated quarterly, so that, like at Chris's federation of schools, the feedback loops between action and learning are much tighter.

It is not only users whose shared wisdom and insight is being used to drive service improvement. John Lewis Partnership, among others, also treat their staff as the 'eyes and ears' of their organisation. They are the people closest to customers, and from their interactions in store they can offer deep insights into how to improve performance from the perspective of people's experiences. Staff are encouraged to share what they learn about customers and their responses to products with colleagues locally, and their views are fed back to product development teams. BUPA also worked to underline the importance of employees providing feedback as they developed their excellence profiles. Alison Platt told us: 'We had to get away from the culture of "I just want to do my job". Well actually, feedback *is* your job.'

Service innovators do not ask only people-facing staff to offer insights back to the organisation. They also ensure that managers and senior staff have a direct line to the interface. This is not about 'visits' or 'inspections'; to be effective these organisations have looked for ways of putting the customer squarely on the board's agenda. As one respondent told us, 'they've got to feel it'. BUPA involves all senior staff in the work around user journeys. In addition, every week the directors take on ten customer complaints and have to sort them out. This is about real exposure, not visits.

Closing the gap between information and users

Paul Hodgkin is a practising GP who has a sideline in an exciting new social enterprise. In 2005 he founded the website www.patientopinion.org.uk. It is a brilliant example of how service innovators are creating new channels at the interface that bring together feedback, service measurement and user information simultaneously. The website invites people who have recently experienced hospital treatment to swap stories. Other people preparing to go to hospital can use the site to help them make decisions about where to go for their treatment; the information is far more accessible and immediate than any star rating or performance report. Paul also sells full access to the information on the site to primary care trusts, to enable them to get a better feel for system performance from a different perspective. In effect, looking at the website gives the trusts continuous access to 'collective wisdom across the system'. Patient Opinion's strapline is 'this is our NHS . . . let's make it better'.

Like Chris Gerry's feedback tools, it is not possible to separate out insight, measurement, feedback and information on Paul's website. Chris's and Paul's work illustrates a wider pattern that

we detected across other successful service organisations we spoke
to. Increasingly, feedback, insight and ideas are things that are
not only gathered, but also offered back to users of services.
Service innovators are looking for ways to open up and break down
the barriers between customers and organisations. They see every
interaction between a person and the service as an opportunity to
learn something new.

Requesting and sharing information and insight on a regular
basis offers an effective new channel of honest dialogue that can
benefit service organisations and users in equal measure. Presenting
system information and measurement back to users in accessible
and usable ways is an important element of building trust and
putting people in control. For example, if district-level data suggests
that crime is going down, but a person knows that burglaries have
gone up on their street, they are unlikely to believe the figures.
Providing street-level data on crime would help people to close the
gap between service experiences and system measures. It would give
people the confidence that their local police force had enough data
and insight to target specific problem areas. Improved technology
should make this kind of 'very local' information and insight
gathering possible in a way it would not have been 20 years ago.

These organisations are pioneering an approach that combines
service delivery, service design and insight generation at the point
of the interface, to inform policy and ongoing system re-design.
There is much that can be learnt here for future public services.
Politicians and policy-makers are searching for a new way of looking
at performance that takes in trust and satisfaction. It seems unlikely
that ever more fine-grained system measurements (eg customer
satisfaction, value added) will provide the solution. Instead, we need
to look at how experiences are measured and assessed, and put
these insights alongside some of the more abstract measures already
in existence.

Adding in experience metrics and reducing feedback loops will
help to tackle the deep problems of mistrust and dissatisfaction.
There is an additional benefit too. As this chapter has outlined,

smaller feedback loops are a key element in creating a culture of experimentation and innovation. The service innovators we spoke to learnt from getting it wrong, but they learnt quickly and were able to adapt and improve quickly thanks to their deeper understanding of the impact of particular decisions and approaches. For these organisations, a formalised service design development methodology mitigates the risk of failure by managing incremental levels of service prototyping. Involving users at every stage also enables service designers to spot flaws not just in terms of operational systems, but also in terms of the experience of users.

Challenges

+ How are you measuring the experience of different kinds of users?

+ How frequently are you assessing performance against experience metrics?

+ Is your organisation ready to use feedback, even if it is negative?

+ What access do your users and staff have to performance information? Is it presented in an accessible format that communicates to people at their level of interest?

+ Are you benefiting from the collective wisdom of your customers?

A shared language of service

Experience metrics
My-metrics
Collective wisdom
Prototyping

Definitions on pages 107–108

Young people in Kensington and Chelsea

'It's unusual to find good working relationships at this level,' says Isobel Rickard, who lives in Lincolnshire but spends her working week running housing management services for Kensington and Chelsea Tenant Management Organisation. She is pioneering a new approach to tackling anti-social behaviour that stands out from the rest.

For one thing, her view of 'rolling out' is not about determining how things should be and telling others to deliver services differently: 'It's hard to sit round as managers and say it needs to happen – it needs to come from the bottom up.' Instead, Isobel is working with the council's Youth and Education Welfare Services, and the local police, to build the crucial relationships estate by estate. Together they are creating estate-level partnerships, based on trust and a shared sense of purpose, which take in voluntary organisations, registered social landlords and the numerous other agencies that play some part in tackling anti-social behaviour: 'you've got to look at the whole picture'.

You get the sense that much has been learnt from the perspectives of different professions on the same sets of issues. This understanding has been crucial to orchestrating the integrated service that Isobel and her team are working to create. The Tenant Management Organisation (TMO) got involved in training the community police support officers, and they have played a huge part in some of the local successes. The TMO also works very closely with the youth service, which provides outreach work in some of the problem areas. This has created a sense of 'common endeavour . . . bringing all those people together made it possible to see how they could all make some changes.'

An important turning point was the success of the collaboration between the police and the TMO in pinpointing and closing down a number of crack houses in the borough. In one area this joint working saw the successful removal of five major dealers and massive reductions in crime – car theft by 50 per cent, street violence by 60 per cent and burglary by 30 per cent. 'The police found that there was a huge pay-off in working with us, and that's really important. There's got to be a pay-off; everyone's got to get something out of it.'

However, it is not just partnerships that have made the model so successful. Isobel has also stressed the importance of giving a voice to young people, so often demonised in discussions of anti-social behaviour. For example the TMO, youth service and police carried out a consultation exercise on one estate to gain a better understanding of the perspective of young people. The result was a series of activities delivered by all the different agencies, which enabled staff to get to know the kids by name and build relationships with them. This is about involving young people in designing services. 'We have to fit around them even if we don't always agree,' says Isobel. 'They need to know the estates, know where the trouble will be.'

Although this approach may sound like common sense, Isobel has clearly fought hard: 'Selling the idea of financing bad behaviour will always be hard.' Nevertheless, she has stood firm. She sees anti-social behaviour orders (ASBOs) as impossible to enforce – 'so what's the point?' – and as a result there are only three ASBOs in the borough. 'There's so much money out there being spent on anti-social behaviour but it's all going on the punitive stuff. Why don't we put some into prevention as well?' This belief does not stop intervention, far from it: 'Of course we intervene as soon as we identify a problem – but we're not heavy handed, we let the voluntary workers do their work first.'

Working at an estate level has enabled the teams to see the importance of improving relationships on estates, building the capacity to manage and co-exist peacefully, rather than simply trying to tackle or contain anti-social behaviour. It is an approach that has been applied across the TMO's estates – for example a recent exercise at World's End saw older people gathering in hoods and baseball caps while young people tried getting about with canes and walking frames.

The professionals involved and the attitudes they bring with them really matter: 'The quality of individuals in tackling this stuff is paramount.' This does not necessarily mean working only with experienced or fully trained staff: the TMO has introduced a graduate trainee scheme, taking on people with no housing experience and giving them the opportunity to study for an MA in housing while working. Four young people have been trained through the scheme in the last two years – and one has just become an area manager.

What's also striking about Kensington and Chelsea's approach is the emphasis it places on regular feedback, which is regarded as crucial and is firmly focused on operations. Every week the agencies involved – registered social landlords, the police, environmental health, the TMO, mediation services, victim support, the youth offending team and the domestic violence team – meet for a quick-fire exchange of information. This is vital, according to

Isobel, 'so that nothing's happening that no one knows about'. The meetings offer a way of exchanging information early and making connections. They also enable staff to track particular young people, wherever they are and whoever is dealing with them. In the past, says Isobel, the partnership was 'good at doing things initially, but not very good at following through'.

Isobel is adamant about the need for this meeting to be kept to staff at an operational level and has resisted the temptation to use the gathering for training sessions or other activities: 'As soon as things go up into the strategic level then things stop happening – and these meetings have done more for anti-social behaviour than anything else in the last three years.'

It is clear that the TMO's approach is having a dramatic impact, not only on the lives of the young people but also on the overall quality of life on the estates where this approach is being used. For Isobel , this is all that matters: 'Performance indicators have no relevance or meaning at all to what's actually going on here – we'd spend so much time counting that we wouldn't be able to do anything! It's very hard to measure how many people haven't gone on to be in gangs.'

4
The politics of service design

*If applied systemically, service design can
offer a vision for the transformation of public
services, as well as a route to get there.*

The principles of the previous chapters could be used to great
effect to improve existing service organisations. But only if they are
applied systemically will service design principles have the potential
to transform public services as we know them. Service design
approaches help to close the gap between what people want and
need, and what organisations do. It helps to generate a shared, single
view of system priorities that connects actual experiences with
the setting of those priorities. Service design focuses minds on the
deeper purpose of service – to generate deep forms of satisfaction
and wellbeing. And it builds the capacity of organisations and
groups of organisations to adapt and morph as people's needs
change. In these terms, service design can offer a vision for
transformation, as well as a set of tools and a model of change
for bringing it about.

Current models of service have created a distinctive set of building blocks for public services – functional institutions, episodes and abstract system or output measurements. The approach taken to reform is itself driven by these building blocks: they produce an agenda that is focused on very particular models of the core elements that any political party in power would need to address in thinking about public services. For example, a view of services as commodities encompasses the following assumptions:

- *Efficiency* is seen to be primarily about increasing the capacity of the existing system to do more. It is about operations, driving out bureaucracy and tightening existing processes and supply chains. For example, the Gershon review of 2004 indicates that cuts of £20 billion are going to be achieved through a combination of cutting 'inputs' (mainly jobs) and increasing 'productive time'.[34]
- *Personalisation* is equated most often with consumer models of mass customisation, where particular services are modularised and people are able to choose – but not always co-design – services. For example, the education white paper of 2005 made proposals about school choice, and the creation of 'choice advisers' to help parents navigate a complex and hard-to-read system.[35] Patients can now choose from a range of treatment centres (not all state-run) for where they access their treatment.
- *Devolution* to the frontline is accompanied by checks and measures to ensure that the local authorities and service organisations are responding to an agenda that remains predominantly set by the centre. Peter Taylor-Gooby has characterised this kind of devolution as a 'principal–agent' relationship.[36] For example, inspections are carried out by semi-independent organisations such as Ofsted on behalf of the centre, and local authorities continue to be measured primarily against systemic targets. Limited metrics of customer satisfaction have been introduced as a counterweight but, in the main, central targets still drive assessments of performance.

Service design re-frames the central tenets of any reform agenda

The language and frameworks that we use determine the parameters of the debate, and limit the kinds of organisational and service innovations that we can imagine. Service designers do not see service as something that can be reduced to a commodity: they understand it instead as being a form of support, a kind of scaffolding to help people live their lives as they wish. By offering a fresh set of building blocks – the touchpoints, journeys, channels, service environments and architectures that together form the drivers for change in every service organisation we spoke to – service design re-frames the ways in which the main elements of reform can be understood.

In focusing on the interaction *between* people and services, rather than services alone, service design enables policy-makers and practitioners to see new possibilities. Far from simply offering incremental improvements to existing services, these possibilities could add up to radical new models of service, organisations and value.

Efficiency

Systems thinkers, health economists and others have for a long time argued that we need a wider view of efficiency than current models allow for. It is not that achieving operational efficiency is not desirable: it's just that it is not the whole picture. Two further forms of efficiency that service design focuses on include:

+ *designing out waste.* It has been estimated that between 30 per cent and 70 per cent of any organisation's time is spent on 'failure demand' – the cost of getting it wrong the first time.[37] These costs are measurable not only in terms of time, but also in staff morale. Finding that the system works against being able to focus fully on meeting people's needs has obvious implications for levels of staff motivation and satisfaction.

- *harnessing and unleashing the untapped resources of users' time, energy and motivation.* By focusing on relationships and experiences, good service design enables policy-makers to create services that *engage* people, services that invite them in to participate in the creation of positive outcomes.

Service design maximises existing resources *and* brings new resources into the equation, as well as seeking to minimise costs.

Challenges

- How can prevention be measured meaningfully – the things that *don't* happen – for example, a teenager resisting pressure to join a gang, or someone eating healthily?
- Can we develop efficiency metrics that consider efficiency over a lifecycle rather than through specific service episodes? We have developed lifetime costings for everything from photocopiers to weapons to cars and washing machines and yet we do not do the same for vital public services.
- Can politicians find the courage to tell a story about efficiency that extends beyond the current political cycle? Can they make the case for investing in public services for the long term, rather than a story that simply focuses on getting the most out of them in the here and now?

Personalisation and co-production

Choice has become the primary mechanism by which this government is seeking to personalise services. It is seen as a means of enabling greater user autonomy, and a way of engaging people in the creation of outcomes.

Of course it is true that the freedom to choose is a crucial part of feeling in control. But making stressful, potentially life-changing choices requires that those decisions are surrounded by dialogue, useful and accessible information, recognition and support. Being asked to choose from a menu of options, none of which appear to reflect your needs and the kinds of social and cultural contexts you are operating within, can be as disengaging and frustrating as a situation where there is no choice at all.

Service design helps policy-makers and service providers to counter this 'choice bias' through opening up new mechanisms and channels for engaging people not only in choosing between services, but also in shaping those services in the first place:

- Service designers use methodologies that start with people, not existing services or institutions. The lifestyle management company TEN UK begins by asking its customers three simple questions: Who are you? What do you want or need (and when, how and where)? How can we help? The organisations, partnerships and forms of support flow from a deep understanding of what those support needs are in the first place. For good service designers, the unit of service is always the person, not the institution, patient, disease, or, worse still, the bed. Service design offers both a conceptual framework *and* a set of tools for politicians and policy-makers seeking to create deeply personalised services.
- Service designers focus on a specific kind of engagement: *engagement at the interface*. Deliberation has to take place at the point of delivery to create the kind of engagement required for co-production – that where people are mobilised, coached, and encouraged to participate in the 'common enterprise' of generating positive outcomes. The current emphasis on 'public engagement' in policy-making circles fails to see and reinforce the vital connection between engagement for co-production and experiences. Whether it is the setting up of foundation hospital boards, the creation of community representative posts on local strategic partnerships, or the current education bill's emphasis on parental involvement in school governance (rather than their children's learning), too often such engagement is seen to happen in town halls, school gyms or conference centres, away from the real action of service experiences. In contrast, service design offers a powerful set of tools by which experiences can be shaped to meet the goal of genuine engagement.

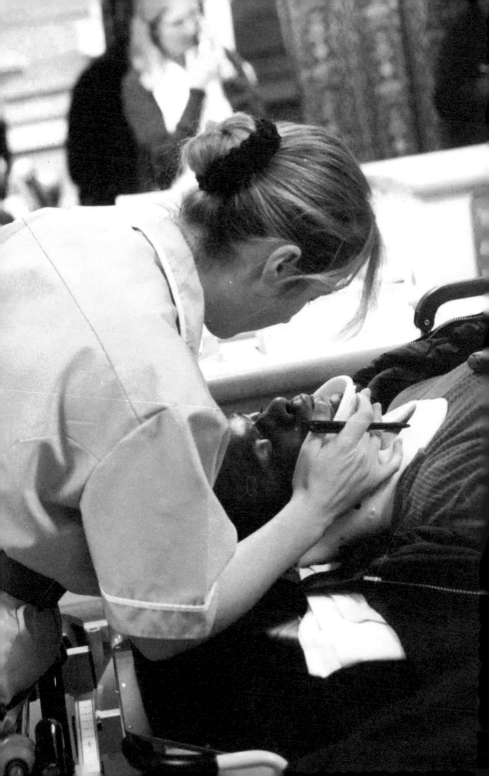

By starting with people themselves, not organisational norms or institutional parameters, and by focusing on engagement at the interface, service design shapes an agenda for personalisation that is about co-design and co-creation rather than mass customisation.

Challenges

+ By starting with people, it will not always be the case that a single organisation can meet that person's needs. What cultural, professional and technological environments and incentives are needed for genuine partnership working? What forms of governance can be developed to enhance a sense of collective endeavour across services and between services and citizens?
+ How can the many 'ways in' to services – the range of channels – be designed to engage and enhance people's experiences of services, as well as simply being seen as a route to more efficient delivery mechanisms?
+ What kinds of data sharing and people-centred knowledge management systems are needed to underpin these more fluid, federating forms of support? Where are the opportunities to learn from the most innovative technological developments in this area?

Devolution

The commitment to devolving power from the centre to the local has been part of the reform agenda since 1997. More recently, the notion of 'double devolution' – where power is devolved from the town hall to the neighbourhood – has become popular in policy-making circles, further emphasising a commitment to create flexible, responsive services appropriate for specific communities and localities.

Devolution and frontline empowerment was certainly a crucial characteristic of all the innovative service organisations we visited; however, it was a very different kind of devolution that we uncovered. For organisations like John Lewis Partnership or BUPA or places like Kensington and Chelsea, the relationship between the centre and the local or the frontline is characterised by trust and a sense of mutual accountability: each holds the other to account for the part they play in the ultimate goal of great service. When applied systemically, service design approaches focus on the ways in which mutual accountability can grow; they shift the emphasis away from the notion of a principal–agent relationship:

- The frontline is held to account for customer satisfaction, loyalty and the provision of good service, defined by customer measures and my-metrics, rather than system goals alone. These expectations are 'designed in' to innovative service organisations in every possible way – through appraisals and performance frameworks, through the stories told to keep the ethos of the organisation alive, through the clear sponsorship of a customer focus from the very top, and in the particular forms of success that are celebrated.

- Service designers seek to create more intimate relationships between services and people. In order to achieve this they create channels for information to flow *upwards* as well as downwards – forms of feedback and insights – which are then used to drive priorities and focus. Part of this is designing in ways in which the frontline can hold the system or the organisation to account for the part they need to play in creating great service. Staff are expected to challenge those systems and processes that are not supporting them in their drive to develop intimate relationships with customers – and this kind of challenge is actively sought out and encouraged. By demanding a focus on the interface, every element of the system is held to account for the part they have to play in maintaining that focus. Service design approaches seek to build in systems of mutual accountability flows to achieve this.

Service designers treat the centre and the frontline as playing an equally crucial but different role in achieving the ultimate goal of great service. But part of great service is shortening and strengthening the feedback loops from the shop floor to the boardroom, from the neighbourhood to the Whitehall department. Service design is a collaborative and recursive process that bridges the gap between the activities of policy-making and the day-to-day activities that are currently called delivery or implementation.

Challenges

+ How can 'evidence-based' policy-making learn to take the insights of practitioners and frontline professionals as seriously as the views of 'experts', academics and management consultants when making decisions?
+ What kinds of channels and feedback loops between the centre and the frontline can be designed in to the early stages of policy formation? How can these approaches add up to more than consultation alone? How can policy itself be 'co-produced'?
+ How can the lateral capacity of the public service system be enhanced? How can we grow spaces where frontline professionals and practitioners can work together, in order to create a system that is able to learn from itself?

Service design offers a model of change and a route to transformation

> *Is there, to use a phrase from a recent Audit Commission document, some 'quantum leap' – perhaps it's the introduction of market disciplines; perhaps reorganisation (shared services), or new techniques for managing customer relations or information flows.*[38]

The treatment of services as commodities not only determines how the elements of the reform agenda are framed; it also shapes the ways in which government and others approach change itself.

Markets have been part of the public service reform narrative for over 20 years now, most recently expressed through the commitment to opening up service provision to a more diverse set of providers from all sectors. Improvement, in these terms, is wrought through increasing contestability, competition and consumer choice. Contractual management, regulation and objective inspection, and performance frameworks are used to drive up standards.

Regardless of whether this emphasis is right or wrong, what underpins it is a more fundamental belief: that change to public services will come about through grafting alternative models and innovations onto existing institutions. Successive administrations have sought to harness the potential of such innovations from other sectors. From meritocracy and professionalisation in the mid-nineteenth century, to mass production, to Thatcher's focus on privatisation, agency-based delivery and contract-based management, and from new public management to consumer models of choice, public services now represent a hybrid of different approaches to change applied at different periods over the last 150 years.

Building adaptive capacity alongside managerial capability

Service design is less interested in taking the models of one sector and overlaying them onto existing models of service. Instead, through harnessing user participation, feedback, insight generation and connecting these things to organisational or system design and development, service design's model of change is focused on creating a system able to continuously adapt, reconfigure and, most importantly, *learn from itself*.

We have already argued that engagement and ultimately participation are vital to co-producing the outcomes that this government is looking to achieve. In that sense, successful and meaningful participation is a goal in itself. However, for service designers, participation brings additional benefits as a *process of learning and change* as well as an outcome.

As the team at the Luton and Dunstable Head and Neck Cancer Unit discovered, participation offers the opportunity of embedding experiences in the process of continuous change, rather than having an intermittent relationship between disjointed consultation exercises and a permanent managerial revolution. Service design offers tools and techniques to build that adaptive capacity, from the generation of particular kinds of data and insights, to the means of connecting these to organisational design and development.

The challenge for policy-makers is to focus on building this adaptive capacity, alongside the current goal of developing better managerial capabilities. While the Capability Reviews announced by Gus O'Donnell in October 2005 may shed some insights into 'how well the service is performing and not by its own measure but by independent, credible, objective assessment',[39] they will not provide government with the tools it needs either to measure adaptive capacity, or to develop it.

Investing in 'in-between spaces' as well as existing institutions
The Prudential took a bold and innovative step in providing Richard Duvall and his team with the space to come up with the concept of the online bank Egg. They realised that their particular model of banking was in decline, and that in the future they would need to find an innovative business model in order to keep their customers and maintain their profit margin. But, equally significantly, they realised that they would find it almost impossible to come up with this fresh model within the constraints of their own organisation. They saw that the power of existing institutional patterns and norms would work against the kind of transformative innovation they were looking for. So instead they set Richard the challenge of coming up with something completely new – through setting him free from all the organisational routines and requirements. The results speak for themselves.

Similarly, Paul Hodgkin believes that his website www.patientopinion.org.uk would not have been devised and developed within the constraints of the NHS. Just like John Proctor in our case study about Birmingham OwnHealth, Paul believes that the most exciting innovations need new platforms and business models in order to learn how such spaces might grow. Although he sees the website as a resource that helps the system as well as individual users, he believes creating it as a social enterprise was an essential factor in the success of his innovation – both in terms of the service he offers, and the business model that underpins it.

It is striking how many of the examples and case studies we found in the course of our research emerged out of these 'in-between spaces' – partnerships and collaborations set up at arm's length from the major public service institutions that are in operation. This pattern is mirrored in innovation literature. Many markets are characterised by a handful of large stakeholders, and a larger number of small enterprises, whose innovations are tested and developed at a manageable scale, before the successful ones get incorporated and integrated into the larger organisations of that sector.

In order to strengthen the system's ability to learn from itself, there is real merit in *investing* in these in-between spaces alongside strengthening the feedback loops between insights and organisational development. They are a means of experimenting, learning and innovating on behalf of the wider system. Much could be learnt from investigating and seeking to understand these collaborative models in more detail and government, both local and central, urgently needs to create opportunities for the development of these spaces.

There are many opportunities for focusing existing innovation funds towards investing in these in-between spaces, whether that's the Invest to Save Budget looked after by the Treasury,[40] or the 'next practice projects' sponsored by the Innovation Unit at the Department for Education and Skills.[41] But in creating spaces beyond organisations to experiment with new models of service, we should not assume that they need to be fully funded by government.

We also found that these collaborative 'in-between' partnerships enable new forms of incentives for user focus to be designed in to the ways in which services are shaped and offered. It is notable that many of the organisations that had successfully closed the gap between what they were offering and what people want and need had partnership, subscription or social enterprise business models. Alongside the commitment in the 2006 Budget to explore the impact of the voluntary sector's role in economic and social regeneration, looking at alternative business models for service organisations could provide a rich seam of insight about how public services can grow and form themselves around the needs of users and citizens.

Service design demands that the unit of service is the person, and that service is devised in collaboration with them in order to fit around their everyday lives. Too often, the power of institutional norms and practices stands in the way of this approach, regardless of sector. Therefore the most likely places to grow capacity for the kinds of user-centred approaches service design advocates appear to be those 'in-between' spaces. It is in these spaces that small organisations are really beginning to define very different notions of service and value. The challenge for policy-makers in these terms is two-fold: first, to find innovative ways of investing in these spaces without legislating for everything that takes place within them; and second, to learn more about how the lessons learnt in these spaces can be 'scaled up' to a system-wide approach.

Challenges

* How can we strengthen the connections between people's experiences of service and system priorities in order to drive greater adaptive capacity? What kinds of metrics are necessary? How can these metrics be built into existing patterns such as inspections, spending reviews, target setting and so on?
* How can the capacity of the system to continuously adapt to the dynamic, uncontrollable and unpredictable nature of human activity be put at the forefront of the debate, rather than managerial capability alone?
* How can the government invest in these 'in-between' spaces without legislating for everything that takes place within them? Beyond the straightforward deployment of existing innovation funds, what other kinds of business models and partnerships might help to grow these spaces to learn about what works?

- How can the lessons learnt from 'in-between' spaces be used to inform changes to institutional models and relationships? How bold are politicians willing to be in taking these lessons to focus future efforts on public service transformation rather than incremental improvements alone?

The politics of service design: a vision as well as a route to transformation

A year into the third term of a Labour government, we are at a point where the terms of the debate around public service reform are in flux. Many principles developed in 1997 – national standards, devolution to the frontline, user focus, contestability – remain central. More have been added since, most notably the idea of 'invest and reform' and a growing interest in what contestability actually looks like in practice, alongside the commitment to greater choice as a means of empowering users.

Where this debate goes next, however, is still an open question. Efficiency is clearly a crucial element of any agenda, as an ageing population and increased expectations place more demands on our public service infrastructure than ever before, while at the same time current levels of investment look unsustainable in the long term.

But there is a growing consensus across the whole political spectrum that managerialism cannot be the sole solution to the transformation of services. The question remains: what are the elements of a reform agenda that can reconnect the activities and priorities of government with the priorities and concerns of the electorate? The opportunity for a powerful story about the importance of service to people's lives is there for the taking; as Cameron's Conservatives begin to tackle public services, the question remains: which party will be the first to seize it?

The recent local elections should be seen at least in part as a kick against incumbency: voters rejected councils that were perceived to have lost sight of the bottom line of service – where user needs and experiences, not targets, drive provision. There can be real and felt differences between system success and the quality of experiences, and citizens are looking for this to be recognised by the politicians they elect. People are tiring of being told that services are improving when their experiences of those same services remain impersonal, and not on their terms. As one campaigner put it, 'people were telling us, make this real for me'.

> The risk element of efficiency (achieving CPA ratings) means that you might get the 3-star CPA ratings but the residents may not think the service is 3-star.[42]

At the heart of the problem with current approaches to public service reform is that the measures in place risk driving a wedge between 'system priorities' and people's experiences of services. Managerial approaches to service create self-sustaining frameworks of determining priorities that do not do enough to take account of feedback from the interface – whether that's through citizens or frontline professionals.

Service design provides a way out of this conundrum. Through its focus on the *interface* between people and services, and the way its methodologies use insights from the interface to drive priorities and organisational change, it offers progressive politicians an opportunity to create a single and unified picture of the system and what needs to happen next. It is through that shared agenda that trust and legitimacy can grow.

The transformation of public services will never emerge from a simple shift in language and warm words about the importance of a user focus alone. Driving reform from the interface out has to grow from a deeper, richer understanding of how people see services. It is from the vantage point of the interface that it is possible to generate a genuinely shared set of priorities and actions that can be used to align every stakeholder across the broad system of public services, from ministers and permanent secretaries to hospital porters. Service design can help politicians, policy-makers and service providers make that long and difficult journey to the interface.

But service design has more to offer than a set of methodologies. The discipline of service design itself grew out of an understanding that services add up to far more than commodities. The value of service lies in the intangible sense that they are supporting you, understanding you, on your side. This is in line with the repeated findings of research which show that people see public services as crucially important, not just in managerial terms, but also in far deeper terms that are about how the state relates to people's lives, and the kinds of values that shape the society in which we live.

It is often said that rational argument is not the most effective way to move agendas on. It is time for politicians to grasp a new narrative of service that is braver and altogether more ambitious. The battle to regain trust and legitimacy, alongside the need to create a sustainable and viable service infrastructure for tomorrow's challenges as well as today's, will not be won through speeding up and intensifying current approaches to reform that, ultimately, continue to treat services as commodities.

There is a parallel here in the recent debates that have been kickstarted about the importance of happiness and wellbeing over and above productivity. A similar debate needs to be led now, and urgently, about how and why public services are so much more than goods to be provided at the lowest cost. The challenges of the future rely on service infrastructures having a whole range of resources – including money, but equally crucial are the resources of trust and legitimacy.

Trust grows out of relationships, which in turn rely on believing people are acting in your interests and telling you the truth. What is needed now is a new story about public services that is rooted in relationships and experiences, in people and in places. The current narrative and its focus on narrowly defined versions of efficiency, personalisation and devolution is out of sync with this. Service design has both the philosophy and the methods that could refocus the debate, and provide politicians with the elements of a more vital, vivid and practical agenda for transformation.

An agenda for action

Service design could focus and refresh many current efforts to improve public services. But its potential needs to be grasped at multiple levels of the system, at the same time, in order to have a powerful effect. Its core revolves around empowering users to play a more active part in shaping what they experience, and therefore in orchestrating more of the 'moving parts' – including people – in a given system to also enhance outcomes.

Government therefore needs to seize this agenda rhetorically and organisationally, and find ways to develop and spread service design approaches within the existing framework of services, rather than trying to impose them from without or implement them solely through existing levers of control.

The opportunities are therefore as follows.

The Treasury should:
* *in the lead-up to the 2007 Comprehensive Spending Review, bring together a diverse working group to explore broader definitions of efficiency and public value*; this group could help to build a critical mass of opinion about richer, long-term understanding of how to measure the impact and value of public service activity
* *support all key service departments and local authorities in developing new metrics that focus on quality of experiences, to go alongside operational and customer satisfaction measures*; in particular, general duties of wellbeing, such as those now carried by local authorities, should be accompanied by regular surveys and feedback systems involving direct user feedback focused on quality and on user confidence, both in themselves and in service providers
* *use the Varney review of service delivery channels to focus on how alternative 'ways-in' to service can bring about better engagement and more positive experiences of public services*; shared services and new information and communications technology interfaces offer great new flexibilities and economies of scale – a new infrastructure for more cost-effective services; but users and citizens must play an integral part in spelling out what

dimensions of services matter to them, and how different channels can work together over time, to guide any further development of the public service infrastructure

* *work with local authorities to explore alternative business models for offering services in the 'in-between spaces' between existing institutions and organisations*; for example, studying local networks of provider organisations, and the 'add-on' services that can emerge beyond their formal function, would uncover many opportunities for service innovation not noticed by national performance reviews; these studies should build on the review and pilots of third-sector involvement in service delivery that are already underway

* experiment, as Egg did, with much *more flexible and intensive neighbourhood-based service models*, possibly via the National Programme for Neighbourhood Renewal; this approach would replace all targets and measurements with a single goal for five years: to meet every person's need; this approach could be piloted in a small and already high-performing area

* work with local authorities and local strategic partnerships to map comprehensively the *unintended consequences of existing targets* – and use these insights to refine and develop targets for the future

* encourage the Lyons Inquiry of local government funding to maintain its focus on 'place shaping';[43] accelerate the development of tools and methods that create shared purpose across diverse groups of people working in public, private and voluntary sectors – users and practitioners – which in turn requires new forms of strategic leadership at local authority level (see Local authorities below)

* through the Lyons Inquiry, find new ways of *emphasising* mutual accountability, for example enabling local authorities to commission the support they feel they need from central government rather than being told which consultants they have to use[44]

* create dedicated seed funding for local authorities and partnerships to *reinvest* in the development of 'in-between spaces' wishing to model new kinds of user-centred and user-led services; this could include a proportion of annual underspend or preventive savings; at a time when public services will need to do more and more, for less money, it is just as important to invest in social innovation as it is in technological innovation.

The Cabinet Office should:
* focus public service leadership training on *system leadership* – the ability and skills to lead that which you do not directly control – which requires trust and legitimacy as well as financial resources
* *build on the Capability Reviews to investigate the extent of 'upwards' flows of information between the frontline and existing Whitehall departments* in order to assess how policy-making can become a collaborative process that bridges the gap between policy development and implementation
* invest in training and development to help civil servants become *specialists in systems and service design*: systems thinking, futures thinking, design methodologies and journey mapping[45]
* *in collaboration with other overarching service organisations, including the voluntary and private sectors, set up a service design school that brings together a multitude of disciplines and offers training for public servants and practitioners;*[46] give this school a research and development function and ensure that its activities in this area adhere to service design principles as well – participatory approaches, collaboration, multidisciplinary teams and prototyping solutions
* *integrate the focus of e-government* with the priorities mentioned above: customer responsiveness, new feedback loops, co-design and co-development of user pathways, and so on
* work with individual spending departments and with the Local Government Association and the Improvement and Development Agency to *establish the scope for using shared audit and feedback*

systems which encourage local integration of different improvement, innovation and performance management regimes.

Delivery departments should:

- *deploy existing innovation funds to support and foster lateral networks of practitioners and frontline providers – and commission these networks to develop responses to long-term issues on behalf of the system*; these networks, not independent experts or consultants, are the people with the expertise required to tackle the most difficult issues
- make it a requirement that *all civil servants at all grades visit the frontline* at least once every six months; senior civil servants should be required to resolve at least ten customer complaints every year
- *develop new feedback channels for frontline staff to shape service mechanisms and infrastructure*, for example through the greater use of online discussion forums, or through consultations that happen before decisions are made, not after
- *worry less about citizen engagement through new structures and forums, and more about engagement at the point of delivery*: make this the focus of public engagement activity and communicate that clearly as a priority for the centre as well as for local government and local service organisations.

The Audit Commission and other inspection bodies should:

- *further develop the system's capacity for self-regulation alongside ongoing audit and inspection*, for example by offering training to leaders of service organisations and reporting on the capacity of local authorities to respond to user feedback and mobilise wider networks of users and service organisations for service re-design
- work with local authorities and HM Treasury to review metrics (see Treasury above)
- *devise new approaches to auditing the governance of the partnerships through which outcomes and objectives will increasingly be achieved* in recognition of the fact that often such outcomes will emerge

from the combined efforts of a number of local bodies, irrespective of their formal responsibilities for particular elements of service provision

✦ be aware that as local councils focus increasingly on 'place shaping' rather than service provision alone, their *ability to commission services on the basis of public value* will be critical to their ability to create a service infrastructure that can generate long-term positive outcomes; the Audit Commission and other inspection and regulatory bodies must develop new ways of assessing this capacity to commission services that are fit for purpose and maximise people's life chances

✦ *hold central government to account to the same extent as local government is held to account*: they are both players in a single system that needs to be focused on great service and support where people need it; central government cannot be seen as hovering 'above' the system – it is part of it

✦ *place a requirement on themselves (the Audit Commission and other inspection bodies) to see their audience not only as service organisations, but also as citizens looking for feedback and information on services*; being given accessible, usable information is a crucial step in building trust and in empowering people to make decisions

✦ *invest in technological innovations to make the provision of the information real-time*: it is only in this way that citizens will really be able to use the information provided to navigate services.

Local authorities should:

✦ *set up a team responsible for looking after customer experiences* – and give it the power to report directly to the senior team of the local authority, so that customer experiences and insights play a central role in setting priorities

✦ *create, in collaboration with citizens, a set of personas* based on sophisticated forms of segmentation combined with journeys, touchpoints and relationship maps

- *add to existing requirements to measure customer satisfaction through developing richer metrics of experience*; for example, measure the success of services in inviting, encouraging and enabling people to participate; use the findings of this research to shape strategic plans and prioritisation
- *use personas and other service design techniques to drive the strategy around shared services* – to ensure that back-office integration does not simply create greater efficiencies but also focuses on offering better experiences that suit the needs and attitudes of different citizens
- experiment with *multidisciplinary teams* that include users and professionals as the team at Luton and Dunstable did
- *prioritise the development of 'very local' data* – for example about crime and grime, 'greening' and so on – that is presented accessibly so that people can see what service improvements mean for them at a neighbourhood or street level, as a means of fostering trust and greater faith in the system
- focus on developing *career structures and compensation packages* which incentivise and focus progression on innovating to create great service experiences, engaging people in the design of services, working collaboratively with users
- *commission services on the basis of a consistently applied, collaboratively developed 'public value' framework* – which does not simply seek out the services offered for the lowest cost, as if they were commodities – but instead focuses on building public trust and engagement through the provision of positive and engaging experiences – whichever sector is delivering the service
- *support the development of expert user groups and networks, across local communities*, and link them together through local consultation and information strategies.

Service delivery organisations (eg schools, hospitals) should:

- *develop forms of governance that, by their nature, drive greater engagement*; for example, schools could devolve 1 per cent of their budget to parents in order to encourage them to collaborate more,not only with the school but also with each other to determine how best to invest that budget[47]
- focus on *mapping their users' journeys* – not only from the point at which that person comes into contact with the institution but from the point at which a child is interested in learning, or from when someone feels unwell
- use these maps to *prioritise activity* and management decisions; use them to shape a *strategy for key partnerships and collaborations* that need to be put in place – so that working together is about working smarter not harder
- *work with users every quarter to review the things that are working least well* and engage those users in helping to identify solutions or approaches that can be prototyped and reviewed
- *give staff permission to experiment and fail* – but make sure that something is learned every time, and manage the risks of experimentation through shortening and tightening feedback loops, and strengthening a culture of openness
- *treat expenditure on support to user-led support and development groups as an investment*: the more spaces and places created for user involvement in service design and delivery, the more resources that are released into the system.

A shared language of service

Journeys
Services don't happen in a vacuum and focusing on touchpoints alone would not enable service providers and service designers to see how each of those touchpoints interact with people's wider lives. For example, a service design approach for a hospital would start, not at the point the patient enters the hospital, but instead at the point at which someone started to feel unwell. Tracing the person's journey over time enables service providers to reflect on the effectiveness and appropriateness of each intervention and service touchpoint in the context of that person's wider life.

Channels
Recent years have seen the expansion of the ways in which people can find services. Rather than visiting a GP, people now have the option of calling NHS Direct, visiting a drop-in medical centre, or checking out their condition online. Understanding the interaction between these channels, when each is used, as well as what each one looks like, is another important element of being able to see the service from a person's perspective.

Segmentation
The problem in public services organisations and local authorities lies less with a paucity of data and more with how that data are used. A range of techniques and increasingly powerful data sources are available that can help an organisation to take raw data and turn it into insights about its users. The sophisticated segmentation approach that Tesco uses goes well beyond mapping the demographic and social status of its customers; it also maps preferences, attitudes and beliefs. This in turn enables Tesco to tailor its offer ever more accurately to its customers.

Proposition
The notion of a proposition puts the onus on the provider to 'package up' a service that is useful, useable and desirable and to place it into the market without any assumption that the audience knows the value of the service on offer or how to access it. The assertion of a proposition states the purpose of a service in terms of the benefits to users.

Designing a service proposition extends beyond the content of the offer to an understanding of how its audience would like to engage with and use a service – and the emotional journey that each user will need to take in order to benefit from it.

Touchpoints

Touchpoints are the tangible elements of service – everything that a person accessing the service sees, hears, touches, smells and interacts with. Recent trends in branding have focused less on logos and design, and more on these touchpoints and how every single touchpoint can 'live the brand' of any organisation. In public services, given the current focus on personalisation, the 'brand' might lead to the question: 'Does every touchpoint of my service empower the user to work with us to achieve the desired outcome?'

Architectures

Service designers see services not as static but as dynamic architectures of dialogues, systems, procedures, resources and so on – through which people have experiences and achieve outcomes. Touchpoints, journeys and channels tell us that we need to see these experiences as users do – as a series of critical encounters that take place over time. Using design techniques to visualise this complex picture often represents a turning point for organisations focused on improving their services: it helps people to see where the priorities are and where the service can be improved.

Service environments

The idea of a service environment extends beyond the built environment to encompass any space and place in which service takes place. Increasingly, websites and the tiny screens on mobile phones are spaces within broader service environments. Seeing the building in which service takes place as a service environment can be a valuable conceptual step to make. Many schools, for example, don't see themselves as service providers and therefore don't see their schools as service environments – this may become increasingly necessary as the role of a school extends to offer other services.

Personas

In designing new services, many organisations will use their customer insights to create a series of personas – or archetypes – and experiment with how they might interact with the service or the architectures of the service environment. This helps to refine and improve what's being offered. Creating 'real' people can really animate discussions and enable service providers to engage emotionally as well as rationally with their users. The methodology of personas can also be used to better understand the experiences and needs of staff.

Guardians of the customer experience

Service innovators invest in the design of people's jobs – and the systems that surround them – to ensure that frontline staff are free and supported to act as guardians of the customer experience. This role isn't limited to frontline staff. As one contributor from Orange told us: 'Even the engineers maintaining the network and the finance guys who determine the tariffs we offer have an effect on our ability to deliver a great service to customers – they need to be aware of the impact of their job on customer satisfaction.'

Mutual accountability

Instead of devolution being accompanied by a series of incentives, checks and balances to ensure that every part of the system is encouraged to focus on the key issues as set by government, mutual accountability demands that those at all levels of service hold each other to account for achieving the principal goal of high-quality and effective service to users – accountability flows in both directions. In this collaboration, frontline staff are not held to account on the performance of the system primarily, but instead, on the satisfaction of users and the quality of the experience. Similarly, frontline staff have a range of channels by which they can hold the centre to account on the effective design of large-scale systems and processes to support an unstinting focus on successful experiences for users.

Excellence profiles

Beyond job descriptions – excellence profiles describe service roles in terms of aspirations, values and behaviours that can guide staff to deliver quality service. To be excellent means to understand in very practical ways what it means to do your job well. They are designed to enable organisations to distribute the responsibility for holding people to account on offering excellent service through being treated as an open resource freely accessible to anyone in the organisation.

Communities of practice

Communities of practice bring together people with shared expertise or experiences from across conventional organisational boundaries. Such communities learn together through action and in doing so build the capacity of all the organisations involved to innovate locally. Supporting such lateral learning opportunities releases the potential for knowledge to be shared across organisations and silos and supports the shift towards creating systems that can learn from themselves.

Experience metrics

Experience metrics are derived through research with users and help organisations to design and measure the performance of a service against what people – rather than their organisation – value. Experience metrics are not measures of high-level outcomes but of the quality of the experience at the interface (see also My-metrics).

My-metrics

There isn't a single debate about public service reform where targets are not criticised for creating unintended consequences. However, arguably, it is not the targets themselves, but what they are focused on that is the cause of the problem. Some of the most successful customer-focused service organisations create targets *with* and *for* their users. These my-metrics are then used to assess the performance of the service as an important counterpoint to other operational measures.

Collective wisdom

In his book, *The Wisdom of Crowds: Why the many are smarter than the few*, James Surowiecki explores the science of engaging communities of interest, rather than individual experts in creating new insights and knowledge.[48] The collective wisdom of crowds is already exploited by software businesses that have recognised that they alone can't keep up with the rate of change in technology and have implemented platforms and principles – not solutions – and engaged their community of users to determine, build and refine what is needed.

Prototyping

People's needs are complex; services need to be able to respond to that complexity rather than seek to drive it out. Trying to get everything right first time at scale is a terrifying prospect in this context. Instead, as the founder of the online bank Egg said, 'I learnt most from getting it wrong, wrong and wrong again'. Prototyping – an approach that informs every design-led project – at a small scale is a means of managing risk and learning from doing. Storyboards are examples of very early prototypes.

Relationship maps

Services are configured from touchpoints, systems and resources but they are brought to life by the dynamic relationships between individuals, communities and organisations – and influenced by the wider social context. Mapping the critical relationships between people that animate an existing service allow those designing it to understand which are working, which are not – and why – and to begin to identify the important journeys and procedures that have, over time, come to drive the quality of these relationships. Through this process, opportunities emerge to make change happen.

Moments of truth

Service designers work with users to understand the critical moments of truth of a service experience – the moments shape peoples' perceptions and responses. These moments of truth can be as simple as the confirmation that an application for a benefit has been successful – or as complex as the experience of a victim of a violent crime hearing the sentencing of their attacker. Many of these moments of truth are un-designed – a resident seeing yet more graffiti on a wall in their street might decide that the local council has given up on dealing with anti-social behaviour in their neighbourhood. The points at which a person most depends on a provider are often the very points at which the provider performs least well – and it's at these moments that someone, disheartened and frustrated, may walk away from that service never to return.

People we spoke with

Greg Beales	*Prime Minister's Delivery Unit, Cabinet Office*
Paul Bello	*Customer Experience Manager, Orange*
Prof. Bernard Crump	*NHS Institute for Innovation and Improvement*
Sean Blair	*Design Strategist*
Martin Bontoft	*Design Strategist*
David Brindle	*The* Guardian *Newspaper*
Andy Carroll	*Change Strategy Team, The Pensions Service*
Alex Cheatle	*Chief Executive, TEN UK*
Cass Chideock	*Cabinet Office*
Chris Downs	*Director, live|work*
Chris Gerry	*Head, New Line Learning Federation*
Peter Gilroy	*Chief Executive, Kent County Council*
Richard Grice	*Head of Strategy and Policy, Improvement and Development Agency*
Paul Hodgkin	*Patient Opinion*
Claire Hutchinson	*Marketing team, Eurostar*
Nick Jones	*Cabinet Office*
Nick C Jones	*PricewaterhouseCoopers*
William Jordan	*Comprehensive Spending Review team, HM Treasury*
Andrew Knott	*PricewaterhouseCoopers*
Duncan Lampard	*Director, PricewaterhouseCoopers*
Jackie Lee-Joe	*Head of Brand Experience, Orange*
Joel Levy	*Head of Strategy, Penn Schoen Berlande (London)*
Patrick Lewis	*Supply Chain Director, John Lewis Partnership*
Seema Malhotra	*Management Consultant, PricewaterhouseCoopers*
Jim Maxmin	*Author*
David Mercer	*Head of Design, British Telecom*
Alison Miller	*Local Government Association*
Adam Morgan	*Director, Eatbigfish*
Oona Muirhead	*Local Government Association*
David North	*Director of Public Affairs, Tesco*
Greg Nugent	*Head of Marketing, Eurostar*
William Perrin	*Cabinet Office*
Alison Platt	*Head of BUPA Hospitals*
Alexander Popple	*Network Intelligence Manager, MSN UK*
John Proctor	*Pfizer Health Solutions/Birmingham OwnHealth*
Isobel Rickard	*Kensington and Chelsea Tenant Management Organisation*
Clive Schlee	*Pret a Manger*
Andrew Sheffield	*Cabinet Office*

Peter Simpson	*first direct*
Owen Smith	*Pfizer Global Pharmaceuticals*
Roy Stephenson	*Cabinet Office*
Angus Struthers	*Service Design Manager, Virgin Atlantic*
Deborah Szebeko	*thinkpublic ltd*
John Thackara	*Author*

Seminar 1: Exploring a new language for the design of services

Andrea Baron	*Policy Adviser, Audit Commission*
Clive Blair-Stevens	*National Social Marketing Centre for Excellence*
Martin Bontoft	*Design Strategist*
Dan Dixon	*Headshift*
Kate Dowling	*Service Designer, Engine*
Eddie Gibb	*Demos*
Richard Grice	*Head of Strategy and Policy, Improvement and Development Agency*
Valerie Hannon	*Director of the Innovation Unit, Department for Education and Skills*
Nick Jones	*Cabinet Office*
Nick C Jones	*PricewaterhouseCoopers*
Oliver King	*Director, Engine*
Andrew Knott	*PricewaterhouseCoopers*
Duncan Lampard	*Director, PricewaterhouseCoopers*
William Perrin	*Cabinet Office*
Ben Reason	*Director, live|work*
Jonathan Slater	*Prime Minister's Delivery Unit, Cabinet Office*
Deborah Szebeko	*thinkpublic ltd*
Jennie Winhall	*Design Strategist, Design Council*

Seminar 2: The common challenge of service

Paul Bello	*Customer Experience Manager, Orange*
Andy Carroll	*Change Strategy Team, The Pensions Service*
Alex Cheatle	*Chief Executive, TEN UK*
Chris Gerry	*Head, New Line Learning Federation*
Adam Heathfield	*Head of Government Relations and Corporate Affairs, Pfizer Global Pharmaceuticals*
Claire Hutchinson	*Marketing team, Eurostar*
Duncan Lampard	*Director, PricewaterhouseCoopers*

Lynne Maher — *Head of Service Innovation, NHS*
Seema Malhotra — *PricewaterhouseCoopers*
Lyn McDonald — *Head of Change Strategy, The Pensions Service*
David Mercer — *Head of Design, British Telecom*
Greg Nugent — *Head of Marketing, Eurostar*
Alexander Popple — *Network Intelligence Manager, MSN UK*
Ed Straw — *Partner, PriceWaterhouseCoopers*
Deborah Szebeko — *thinkpublic ltd*
Martin Vowels — *Ispeaktoyou*

Seminar 3: The journey to the interface for local government

Alison Adams — *Consultation Manager, Hertfordshire County Council*
Jill Bailey — *City of London*
Lindsay Barker — *Head of Corporate Services, Colchester Borough Council*
Sarah Bird — *Older People and Disability Project Manager, Department of Health*
Joy Brindle — *Assistant Chief Executive, Easington District Council*
Geoff Brown — *Head of Performance Improvement, Hertfordshire County Council*
Brigitte Gohdes — *Head of Strategy and Policy, London Borough of Camden*
David Hilson — *Leeds City Council*
Philip Hume — *Head of Policy, Kirklees Metropolitan Borough Council*
Sue Hyde — *Head of Communications and Design, Dorset County Council*
Joanna Killian — *Director of Policy, Resources and Performance, Essex County Council*
Chris Naylor — *Head of Customer First, London Borough of Hammersmith & Fulham*
David Parry — *Head of Public Affairs, St Helens Metropolitan Borough Council*
Balraj Sandhu — *Home Office*
Peter Savage — *Assistant Chief Executive, London Borough of Hammersmith & Fulham*

Notes

1   See www.rsa.org.uk/events/textdetail.asp?ReadID=656 (accessed 5 Jun 2006).

2   See *Budget 2006*, available at www.hm-treasury.gov.uk/budget/budget_06/ bud_bud06_index.cfm (accessed 5 Jun 2006).

3   Presentation by Ben Page, 'Understanding trust in a "show me" world', MORI/ Demos seminar, Apr 2006.

4   U Beck, *Risk Society: Towards a new modernity* (London: Sage, 1992).

5   M Willmott and W Nelson, *Complicated Lives: Sophisticated consumers, intricate lifestyles, simple solutions* (London: John Wiley and Sons, 2003).

6   S Zuboff and J Maxmin, *The Support Economy: Why corporations are failing individuals and the next episode of capitalism* (New York: Viking Adult, 2002).

7   W Hutton, 'Are you being served?', *Observer*, 9 Oct 2005, see http://observer. guardian.co.uk/columnists/story/0,,1735352,00.html (accessed 5 Jun 2006).

8   P Cullum, *The Stupid Company: How British businesses throw away money by alienating customers* (London: National Consumer Council, 2006), see www. ncc.org.uk/publications/stupid_company.pdf (accessed 5 Jun 2006).

9   S Goss, 'The reform of public service reform', *Renewal* 12, no 2/3 (2005).

10 See P Gershon, *Spending Review 2004: Releasing resources for the frontline: Independent review of public sector efficiency* (London: HM Treasury, 2004), available at www.hm-treasury.gov.uk/spending_review/spend_sr04/ associated_documents/spending_sr04_efficiency.cfm (accessed 11 Jun 2006); and M Lyons, 'Lyons Inquiry into local government', available at www. lyonsinquiry.org.uk/ (accessed 11 Jun 2006).

11 P Taylor-Gooby, 'Trust vs efficiency: why is it that the NHS can deliver the goods, and yet still not command public trust?', *Prospect* (Apr 2006), see www. prospect-magazine.co.uk/article_details.php?id=7370 (accessed 5 Jun 2006).

12 W Gibson, quoted in *Economist*, 23 Jun 2000.

13 MOSAIC UK, see www.business-strategies.co.uk/Content.asp?ArticleID=566 (accessed 6 Jun 2006).

14 J Murphy, speaking at Demos, 11 Apr 2006.

15 Comment at local authority seminar as part of the research for this project, 11 May 2006.

16 Marcus Buckingham, former research chief at Gallup.

17 Virgin brand book, quoted in P Ing, *Living the Brand: How to transform every member of your organisation into a brand champion* (London: Kogan Page, 2001).

18 C Burke and I Grosvenor, *The School I'd Like: Children and young people's reflections on an education for the 21st century* (London: Routledge, 2002).

19 Cabinet Office, *Transformational Government: Enabled by technology*, Cm 6683 (London: Cabinet Office, Nov 2005), see www.cio.gov.uk/documents/pdf/ transgov/transgov-strategy.pdf (accessed 6 Jun 2006).

20 Ibid.

21 See www.guardian.co.uk/drugs/Story/0,2763,961014,00.html (accessed 7 Jun 2006).

22 Of 23,000 people with a long-term health condition. Quoted at Nuffield Trust seminar, 13 Feb 2006.

23 Zuboff and Maxmin, *Support Economy*.

24 H Green and S Parker, *The Other Glass Ceiling: The domestic politics of parenting* (London: Demos, 2006).

25 Speech by T Blair to the Confederation of British Industry, 29 Nov 2005.

26 I Illich, *Deschooling Society* (London: Marion Boyars Publishers, 1970, reissued 2002).

27 D Miliband, speech to *Guardian* Public Services Summit, 2 Feb 2005.

28 C Leadbeater, 'Production by the masses: professionals and postindustrial public services' in J Craig (ed), *Production Values: Futures for professionalism* (London: Demos, 2006).

29 L Bassi and D McMurrer, 'Are skills costs or assets?', *Milken Institute Review* Q3 (2004), quoted in C Humphries, *Skills in a Global Economy* (London: City & Guilds, 2005).

30 S Bevan, M Cowling and L Horner, *Workplace Trends Survey* (London: The Work Foundation, 2004), see www.theworkfoundation.com/publications/authors.jsp (accessed 11 Jun 2006).

31 Also known as the 'stages of change model', the theory is concerned with how people modify 'problem' behaviours or engender positive behaviours. Outcome measures are concerned with the capacity to resist temptations and the ability to make decisions. See www.uri.edu/research/cprc/TTM/detailedoverview.htm (accessed 11 Jun 2006).

32 Department for Constitutional Affairs/PricewaterhouseCooper, Research on the consumer experience of the civil justice system, 2004 (unpublished).

33 FF Reichheld, 'The one number you need to grow', *Harvard Business Review* 81, no 12 (2003).

34 See Gershon, *Spending Review 2004*.

35 Available at www.dfes.gov.uk/publications/schoolswhitepaper/pdfs/DfES-Schools%20White%20Paper.pdf (accessed 8 Jun 2006).

36 Taylor-Gooby, 'Trust vs efficiency'.

37 See J Seddon, *Freedom from Command and Control: A better way to make the work work* (Buckingham: Vanguard Education Ltd, 2003).

38 *Guardian Public*, editorial, May 2005.

39 See www.civilservice.gov.uk/reform/capabilities/ (accessed 8 Jun 2006).

40 The Invest to Save Budget is a mechanism to 'encourage innovation and partnership throughout the public sector, in order to improve the efficiency and quality of public services'. See www.isb.gov.uk/hmt.isb.application.2/ (accessed 11 Jun 2006).

41 See www.standards.dfes.gov.uk/innovation-unit/investigation/nextpractice_main/?version=1 (accessed 11 Jun 2006).

42 Comment from local authority interviewee on comprehensive performance assessment (CPA) ratings.

43 The Lyons Inquiry is looking at the function, future role and funding of local government. It published its latest findings on 8 May 2006. See www.lyonsinquiry.org.uk/ (accessed 11 Jun 2006).

44 See H Lownsbrough and D O'Leary, *The Leadership Imperative: Reforming children's services from the ground up* (Demos: London, 2005).

45 See E Straw, *The Dead Generalist: Reforming the civil service and public services* (Demos: London, 2004).

46 This has also been recommended by Geoff Mulgan, Michael Bichard and Charles Leadbeater.

47 This was a recommendation in J Craig, *Schools Out: Can teachers, social workers and health staff learn to live together* (Demos/ContinYou: London, 2005).

48 J Surowiecki, *The Wisdom of Crowds: Why the many are smarter than the few and how collective wisdom shapes business, economies, societies and nations* (New York: Random House, 2004).

DEMOS - Licence to Publish

THE WORK (AS DEFINED BELOW) IS PROVIDED UNDER THE TERMS OF THIS LICENCE ("LICENCE"). THE WORK IS PROTECTED BY COPYRIGHT AND/OR OTHER APPLICABLE LAW.ANY USE OF THE WORK OTHER THAN AS AUTHORIZED UNDER THIS LICENCE IS PROHIBITED.BY EXERCISING ANY RIGHTS TO THE WORK PROVIDED HERE, YOU ACCEPT AND AGREE TO BE BOUND BY THE TERMS OF THIS LICENCE. DEMOS GRANTS YOU THE RIGHTS CONTAINED HERE IN CONSIDERATION OF YOUR ACCEPTANCE OF SUCH TERMS AND CONDITIONS.

1. Definitions

a **"Collective Work"** means a work, such as a periodical issue, anthology or encyclopedia, in which the Work in its entirety in unmodified form, along with a number of other contributions, constituting separate and independent works in themselves, are assembled into a collective whole. A work that constitutes a Collective Work will not be considered a Derivative Work (as defined below) for the purposes of this Licence.

b **"Derivative Work"** means a work based upon the Work or upon the Work and other pre-existing works, such as a musical arrangement, dramatization, fictionalization, motion picture version, sound recording, art reproduction, abridgment, condensation, or any other form in which the Work may be recast, transformed, or adapted, except that a work that constitutes a Collective Work or a translation from English into another language will not be considered a Derivative Work for the purpose of this Licence.

c **"Licensor"** means the individual or entity that offers the Work under the terms of this Licence.

d **"Original Author"** means the individual or entity who created the Work.

e **"Work"** means the copyrightable work of authorship offered under the terms of this Licence.

f **"You"** means an individual or entity exercising rights under this Licence who has not previously violated the terms of this Licence with respect to the Work, or who has received express permission from DEMOS to exercise rights under this Licence despite a previous violation.

2. Fair Use Rights. Nothing in this licence is intended to reduce, limit, or restrict any rights arising from fair use, first sale or other limitations on the exclusive rights of the copyright owner under copyright law or other applicable laws.

3. Licence Grant. Subject to the terms and conditions of this Licence, Licensor hereby grants You a worldwide, royalty-free, non-exclusive, perpetual (for the duration of the applicable copyright) licence to exercise the rights in the Work as stated below:

a to reproduce the Work, to incorporate the Work into one or more Collective Works, and to reproduce the Work as incorporated in the Collective Works;

b to distribute copies or phonorecords of, display publicly, perform publicly, and perform publicly by means of a digital audio transmission the Work including as incorporated in Collective Works;

The above rights may be exercised in all media and formats whether now known or hereafter devised. The above rights include the right to make such modifications as are technically necessary to exercise the rights in other media and formats. All rights not expressly granted by Licensor are hereby reserved.

4. Restrictions. The licence granted in Section 3 above is expressly made subject to and limited by the following restrictions:

a You may distribute, publicly display, publicly perform, or publicly digitally perform the Work only under the terms of this Licence, and You must include a copy of, or the Uniform Resource Identifier for, this Licence with every copy or phonorecord of the Work You distribute, publicly display, publicly perform, or publicly digitally perform. You may not offer or impose any terms on the Work that alter or restrict the terms of this Licence or the recipients' exercise of the rights granted hereunder. You may not sublicence the Work. You must keep intact all notices that refer to this Licence and to the disclaimer of warranties. You may not distribute, publicly display, publicly perform, or publicly digitally perform the Work with any technological measures that control access or use of the Work in a manner inconsistent with the terms of this Licence Agreement. The above applies to the Work as incorporated in a Collective Work, but this does not require the Collective Work apart from the Work itself to be made subject to the terms of this Licence. If You create a Collective Work, upon notice from any Licencor You must, to the extent practicable, remove from the Collective Work any reference to such Licensor or the Original Author, as requested.

b You may not exercise any of the rights granted to You in Section 3 above in any manner that is primarily intended for or directed toward commercial advantage or private monetary. compensation.The exchange of the Work for other copyrighted works by means of digital filesharing or otherwise shall not be considered to be intended for or directed toward commercial advantage or private monetary compensation, provided there is no payment of any monetary compensation in connection with the exchange of copyrighted works.

c If you distribute, publicly display, publicly perform, or publicly digitally perform the Work or any Collective Works,You must keep intact all copyright notices for the Work and give the Original Author credit reasonable to the medium or means You are utilizing by conveying the name (or pseudonym if applicable) of the Original Author if supplied; the title of the Work if supplied. Such credit may be implemented in any reasonable manner; provided, however, that in the case of a Collective Work, at a minimum such credit will appear where any other comparable authorship credit appears and in a manner at least as prominent as such other comparable authorship credit.

5. Representations,Warranties and Disclaimer

a By offering the Work for public release under this Licence, Licensor represents and warrants that,to the best of Licensor's knowledge after reasonable inquiry:

  i Licensor has secured all rights in the Work necessary to grant the licence rights here underand to permit the lawful exercise of the rights granted hereunder without You having any obligation to pay any royalties, compulsory licence fees, residuals or any other payments;

  ii The Work does not infringe the copyright, trademark, publicity rights, common law rights or any other right of any third party or constitute defamation, invasion of privacy or other tortious injury to any third party.

b EXCEPT AS EXPRESSLY STATED IN THIS LICENCE OR OTHERWISE AGREED IN WRITING OR REQUIRED BY APPLICABLE LAW,THE WORK IS LICENCED ON AN "AS IS "BASIS, WITHOUT WARRANTIES OF ANY KIND, EITHER EXPRESS OR IMPLIED INCLUDING, WITHOUT LIMITATION,ANY WARRANTIES REGARDING THE CONTENTS OR ACCURACY OF THE WORK.

6. Limitation on Liability.
EXCEPT TO THE EXTENT REQUIRED BY APPLICABLE LAW, AND EXCEPT FOR DAMAGES ARISING FROM LIABILITY TO A THIRD PARTY RESULTING FROM BREACH OF THE WARRANTIES IN SECTION 5, IN NO EVENT WILL LICENSOR BE LIABLE TO YOU ON ANY LEGAL THEORY FOR ANY SPECIAL, INCIDENTAL,CONSEQUENTIAL, PUNITIVE OR EXEMPLARY DAMAGES ARISING OUT OF THIS LICENCE OR THE USE OF THE WORK, EVEN IF LICENSOR HAS BEEN ADVISED OF THE POSSIBILITY OF SUCH DAMAGES.

7. Termination

a This Licence and the rights granted hereunder will terminate automatically upon any breach by You of the terms of this Licence. Individuals or entities who have received Collective Works from You under this Licence,however, will not have their licences terminated provided such individuals or entities remain in full compliance with those licences. Sections 1, 2, 5, 6, 7, and 8 will survive any termination of this Licence.

b Subject to the above terms and conditions, the licence granted here is perpetual (for the duration of the applicable copyright in the Work). Notwithstanding the above, Licensor reserves the right to release the Work under different licence terms or to stop distributing the Work at any time; provided, however that any such election will not serve to withdraw this Licence (or any other licence that has been, or is required to be, granted under the terms of this Licence), and this Licence will continue in full force and effect unless terminated as stated above.

8. Miscellaneous

a Each time You distribute or publicly digitally perform the Work or a Collective Work,DEMOS offers to the recipient a licence to the Work on the same terms and conditions as the licence granted to You under this Licence.

b If any provision of this Licence is invalid or unenforceable under applicable law, it shall not affect the validity or enforceability of the remainder of the terms of this Licence, and without further action by the parties to this agreement, such provision shall be reformed to the minimum extent necessary to make such provision valid and enforceable.

c No term or provision of this Licence shall be deemed waived and no breach consented to unless such waiver or consent shall be in writing and signed by the party to be charged with such waiver or consent.

d This Licence constitutes the entire agreement between the parties with respect to the Work licensed here.There are no understandings, agreements or representations with respect to the Work not specified here. Licensor shall not be bound by any additional provisions that may appear in any communication from You.This Licence may not be modified without the mutual written agreement of DEMOS and You.

DEM☉S

Open access. Some rights reserved.

As the publisher of this work, Demos has an open access policy which enables anyone to access our content electronically without charge.

We want to encourage the circulation of our work as widely as possible without affecting the ownership of the copyright, which remains with the copyright holder.

Users are welcome to download, save, perform or distribute this work electronically or in any other format, including in foreign language translation without written permission subject to the conditions set out in the Demos open access licence which you can read at the back of this publication.

Please read and consider the full licence. The following are some of the conditions imposed by the licence:

* Demos and the author(s) are credited;
* The Demos website address (www.demos.co.uk) is published together with a copy of this policy statement in a prominent position;
* The text is not altered and is used in full (the use of extracts under existing fair usage rights is not affected by this condition);
* The work is not resold;
* A copy of the work or link to its use online is sent to the address below for our archive.

Copyright Department
Demos
Magdalen House
136 Tooley Street
London
SE1 2TU
United Kingdom

copyright@demos.co.uk

You are welcome to ask for permission to use this work for purposes other than those covered by the Demos open access licence.

Demos gratefully acknowledges the work of Lawrence Lessig and Creative Commons which inspired our approach to copyright. The Demos circulation licence is adapted from the 'attribution/no derivatives/noncommercial' version of the Creative Commons licence. To find out more about Creative Commons licences go to www.creativecommons.org